Who Killed Franklin Gowen?

Published by

P.H. Campbell
82 Bentley Ave
Jersey City, NJ 07304
201 434 2432
pathcampbe@aol.com

Printed in the United States of America

DEDICATED TO THE MEMORY OF

THE PENNSYLVANIA COAL MINERS

ACKNOWLEDGEMENT

The following have provided invaluable assistance during the research for this book:

The staff of the Library of Congress, the National Archives, The Hagley Museum, St. Charles Seminary, The New York Public Library, the Pottsville Public Library, the Jim Thorpe Public Library, the Luzerne Historical Society, the Rockefeller Archives.

Thanks to the following individuals for their assistance:

Bernie Coleman, Stuart Richardson, Eamon Sweeney, Nora Campbell, Judge John Lavelle.

Special thanks to Howard Crown, Christine Goldbeck, Brian Campbell, and Mary Meaney for reviewing the manuscript and providing suggestions.

CONTENTS

CONTENTS

CONTENTS

INTRODUCTION

Who Killed Franklin Gowen? is an in-depth analysis of the death of Franklin Gowen, whose death in Washington D.C., on December 13, 1889, was characterized as a suicide by the Washington coroner, but believed to be murder by Gowen's immediate family. Gowen's death created a sensation in the national newspapers.

Gowen had been president of the Reading Railroad in the 1870s and during his tenure he had waged war on the WBA, the Pennsylvania coal miners' union, and on a group of Irish mine workers known as the Molly Maguires -- a war whose casualties included a number of mining officials, and the execution of twenty Irish mine workers.[1]

Gowen described his conflict with the unions and the Molly Maguires as a battle to preserve American democracy. In fighting this battle he used Pinkerton agents to infiltrate the Mollys and later had these agents testify against the Mollys in a series of showcase trials which resulted in twenty executions.

Gowen claimed that the Molly Maguires were a terrorist gang which had branches all over the United States and that their goal was to destroy the ability of the nation's businessmen to conduct their business as they saw fit.

The miners' union, however, viewed Gowen as an unscrupulous capitalist who was out to control all aspects of the coal mining industry and to enslave the men who worked for him. They accused him of paying minimum wage to the mine workers in order to maximize company profits, and they said that he had more value on the mules that worked in the mines than they had for the mine workers who put their lives in jeopardy every day.[2]

[1] Patrick Campbell, *A Molly Maguire Story. 1992.*

[2] Kevin Kenny, *Making Sense of the Molly Maguires. 1997.*

Some Irish mine workers fought back against Gowen and other capitalists in the coal regions with sabotage, strikes ... and attacks on mine supervisors.[3]

Gowen was eventually ousted from the Reading, but he established a law practice in Philadelphia whose clients included major business corporations, and he remained prominent in the business and social life of the city.

Many of Gowen's clients were involved in legal disputes with other major corporations, and Gowen frequently filed complaints with the Interstate Commerce Commission in Washington about business practices that he himself had employed when he was president of the Reading.

In spite of his reputation among trade unions and the Irish community as a ruthless union buster, Gowen was highly respected in social and business circles, and indeed there were many among his peers who saw nothing at all wrong with a series of hangings if it helped put rebellious lower classes in their place.

For several years after his departure from the Reading, Gowen prospered as he represented oil and coal companies in litigation, and on occasion the target of his litigation was John D. Rockefeller, who at the time, was trying to acquire a monopoly in the oil industry.

After he left the Reading, Gowen seemed prosperous and reasonably well adjusted to his life as a leading American lawyer, although he still hoped to regain the presidency of the Reading Railroad. But on December 14, 1889 he was found dead in a Washington hotel with a bullet in his head and a gun by his side.

At first, rumor had it that a Molly Maguire had killed him to get revenge for the executions in 1877, but the Washington coroner and Pinkerton manager Robert Linden, who had investigated Gowen's death, insisted that Gowen had committed suicide.

[3] Marvin Schlegel, *The Ruler of the Reading*. 1947

Gowen's family, however, and several members of the Washington police, refused to accept this conclusion. But in spite of their objections, suicide became the official verdict on Gowen's death.

Who Killed Franklin Gowen? examines the evidence presented in the major newspapers that covered the story in 1889. The book also includes an analysis of the evidence provided by several medical examiners who examined the evidence recently. Based on this examination it appears that all the evidence indicates that Franklin Gowen did not commit suicide, and that there had been a conspiracy to cover up this fact.

*

My interest in the Gowen case came about as a direct result of my decision to revise *A Molly Maguire Story,* a book I published in 1992. *A Molly Maguire Story* examined the arrest, trial and execution of Alec Campbell, my great uncle, in Carbon County, Pennsylvania in the 1870s. Campbell had been accused of being involved in the murder of two mine bosses.

In this book I had analyzed the evidence against Campbell and came to the conclusion that much of the evidence had been fabricated by the Pinkertons in order to implicate Campbell, and without this evidence there was no case against my great uncle.

I devoted very little space to Gowen's death in *A Molly Maguire Story,* but I had noted the official verdict of suicide and the Gowen family's unhappiness with this verdict.

When I decided to revise *A Molly Maguire Story,* I thought I would devote some more space to Gowen's death, so I went to the New York Public Library and reviewed copies of the newspaper articles published between December 14 and December 28, 1889 that had given extensive coverage to Gowen's death. [4]

[4]   The New York Public Library, 42nd Street and Fifth Avenue, has an extensive collection of newspapers on microfiche, some dating back to 1790.

Gowen's death had made front page news in major newspapers across the country and there were a dozen articles in each edition of each newspaper covering all aspects of Gowen's death -- scores of articles in all, including interviews with his family, his friends and his business associates.

The murder versus suicide theories were argued in depth in the early coverage of Gowen's death, but gradually the suicide theory promoted by Robert Linden of the Pinkerton Detective Agency was accepted by most newspapers.

As I read the evidence being presented by Linden, and Patterson, the Washington coroner, in support of the suicide theory, I came to the conclusion that this theory had more holes in it than Swiss cheese, and that it appeared that a cover-up had taken place.

It was at this point that I decided to continue to look into Gowen's death and go as far as I could to resolve the many conflicts posed by the evidence.

*

My interest in Gowen's death was personal, because he had been a bogeyman in my family for more than a century and was blamed by my father, my grandfather and my great grandfather for the execution of my great uncle.

I was especially interested in who killed him since I had great aunts and numerous cousins out in the coal regions at that time who also blamed him for the death of Alec Campbell, and all of them had a deep-seated animosity toward Gowen.[5]

---

[5] *The Star,* a Washington D.C. newspaper, devoted a great deal of space at first promoting the idea that Gowen was murdered by the Molly Maguires, but within a few days the newspaper was actively promoting the theory that Gowen had committed suicide. *The Star* issues, December 14-23, 1889.

And when I noted in the newspaper coverage of Gowen's death that the Pinkertons had sent twelve detectives out into the coal regions of Pennsylvania to determine if any Molly or Molly Maguire relative had been involved in Gowen's death, I was determined to find out who the Pinkertons had investigated to see if they thought any of my relatives had been involved.

*

There are frequent incidents in modern times where innocent men are convicted of murder based on false evidence deliberately provided by the police, and some of the victims end up on death row. But *Who Killed Franklin Gowen?* provides an example of an entirely different type of miscarriage of justice, when evidence pointing to murder was ignored, and the victim was characterized as a suicide, even though the evidence suggests he was murdered.

That situation may not have been unique in the annals of crime, but it certainly was very unusual given the high profile of the victim.

PART ONE

Gowen A Suicide?

Franklin Gowen was found dead in Room 57 in the Wormley Hotel in Washington D.C. on December 14, 1889. A bullet had entered his head above and behind his right ear and exited through his left ear. He lay on his back with his feet facing a marble fireplace. His body was fully dressed and his shirt, jacket and underwear were soaked with blood down to his waist. A 38 caliber Smith & Wesson pistol lay by his right hand; the handle of the pistol was covered in blood. A pool of blood formed beneath his head, and two spots of blood were sprinkled on the hearth of the fireplace. A spot of blood was also evident on the floor across the room at the foot of a bureau.[6]

The Wormley Hotel was a first class hotel and its rooms were large and comfortable. An expensive Belgian carpet covered the floor, and a carved writing table and a mahogany chair stood in the middle of the room. The chair was overturned when the body was found, and a lamp, which had been on the table, lay on the floor, unlit. An ornate bed stood in one corner of the room, with an oak wardrobe nearby. The bed had not been slept in, but the covers had a rumpled look. A heavy bureau stood near the bathroom door, and a large marble fireplace, which had a huge mirror over the mantelpiece, dominated the entire room.[7]

Two of the bedroom windows looked out on to an alleyway 30 feet below that separated the hotel from the building owned by the German Embassy.

[6] *Miners' Journal*, Pottsville, PA, December 15, 1889.
   New York Herald, December 16, 1889.
   New York Times, December 15, 1889.
[7] *The Star.* Washington. December 14, 1889.
   The Philadelphia Inquirer, December 15, 1889.

The window shades were drawn down completely and the curtains drawn almost shut, admitting very little daylight -- just enough to see objects in the room once a viewer's eyes became accustomed to the darkness.

The bedroom door leading to the corridor was locked from the inside and the door leading from the bathroom to the outside corridor was also closed and locked.[8]

Gowen had been dead for some time: those who discovered his body said he was cold and stiff and the blood had congealed on the wound. No one claimed to have heard a gunshot.

James Thompson Wormley, owner of the hotel, told a reporter for *The Star* on Saturday afternoon, December 14, that he became alarmed when he was informed by a maid that Room 57 was locked from the inside and there was no response to repeated knocks.

He said the maid had also told him that she had tried to enter the room several times the previous day to make the bed, and on the first two attempts had been refused entry by Gowen, who said he was busy writing and did not want to be disturbed. On three subsequent attempts the maid found the door locked from the inside and no response to her knocks.[9] When she discovered the door locked again at 11:30 AM that morning the lack of response to her knocks alarmed her, and she told Wormley.

Wormley's reaction, according to the reporter, was to contact a policeman named Cross whose beat included the Wormley Hotel. Then, Wormley accompanied by Cross and Preston, the hotel clerk, went to the second floor to Room 57, and Wormley, with the aid of a step ladder, looked through the transom into the room and saw the body of Gowen lying on the floor in front of the fireplace, a gun by his side.

[8] *The Star.* December 14, 1889.
[9] Ibid.

Wormley then had a slightly built member of his staff climb through the transom into the room to open the door.

According to Wormley, there was no question that Gowen was dead and that he had been dead for some time.[10]

Wormley said he then searched the room to see if another person was present, and when he found no one, he said that, based on the fact that the room was locked from the inside and the gun was on the floor near Gowen's body, he thought it reasonable to assume that Gowen had stood in front of the mirror hung over the fireplace, placed the gun to his head and pulled the trigger.

Wormley then requested that Patrolman Cross arrange to have the body moved to the New Jersey Avenue police station, which was only a short distance away.

Within an hour, the body was wrapped in a blanket, and a horse and carriage was used to transport the body from the hotel to the police station.

An hour after the body was removed from the hotel and was laid out on the floor in a back room at the police station, it quickly became an object of curiosity to people in the neighborhood, who were allowed into the station by the police to view the body.[11]

Meanwhile, Wormley had workers come into Room 57 and remove the blood-stained carpet from the floor and remove the wallpaper from the walls. And while this was taking place, he let the reporter from *The Star* into the room and allowed him to sketch the death scene and interview his staff. The reporter's story was in the newspaper within hours and was circulating around Washington even before the Washington Coroner and Gowen's relatives arrived on the scene.[12]

[10] *The Star.* December 14, 1889.
[11] *The Philadelphia Inquirer.* December 15, 1889.
[12] *The Star,* December 14, 1889.

It was this *unnamed* reporter's version of the death of Franklin Gowen that became the basis for the official version of how Gowen died, and it remained the official version even thought it was challenged in the days that followed by prominent personalities who were convinced that the Molly Maguires had killed their old enemy in revenge for the execution of twenty Irish-American mine workers.

The Star version of the death of Franklin Gowen was based on the information provided by James Thompson Wormley, and by *The Star* reporter's personal observations in the Gowen suite. It was a plausible story and it presented the argument that there was no question but that Gowen had committed suicide.

The argument in *The Star* went as follows: Franklin Gowen was found dead in a room in which the bedroom door was locked from the inside, thus, according to *The Star,* providing a murderer with no avenue to make his escape. The weapon used in the suicide lay beside his hand, so the reporter thought it logical to assume that Gowen had used the weapon to take his own life.

The reporter believed that there was no possibility that Gowen's death was the result of murder because a murderer could not have escaped through the locked door, and the only other exit from the room was through the bathroom door leading out into the corridor, but this door was locked and, according to Wormley, the key to the lock was in the hotel office.

According to the reporter, the murderer would never have used the transom to escape because the transom was small and a murderer ran a big risk of being caught if he attempted to wriggle through it. Besides, the porter who opened the transom had said there was dust on the ledge and it was difficult to open, suggesting it had not been opened in a long time.

This left only the two bedroom windows leading out to an alley thirty feet below as a possible means of escape. But Wormley said both of these windows were closed and the reporter examined the ledges of both windows and noted that there were no scuff marks on the ledges, which he believed should have been there if a murderer somehow anchored a rope to an object in the room and then escaped down this rope.

The reporter's conclusion, based solely on the locked bedroom door, was that suicide was the only possible explanation for the death, and this was the verdict that James Thompson Wormley had already arrived at and was being widely accepted in Washington.

The Star version of Gowen's death, which was a dramatic eye-witness report, was picked up by all the newspapers from New York, Philadelphia, and other cities across the country the following day, each putting its own slant on the story, but all basing their coverage on the "facts" presented by *The Star*.

If *The Star* reporter's scenario was the only possible scenario for the death of Gowen, then there would never have been any controversy surrounding Gowen's death. But no sooner had the suicide theory been launched, than there were those who argued that a murder had taken place and that the owner of the hotel was trying to cover it up.

Most vocal of those murder theorists was Cassius M. Anstett, a friend of Gowen's who was also a resident of the Wormley Hotel. Anstett said he knew Gowen better than anyone else and would never believe Gowen took his own life.[13]

[13] *The Star*, December 16, 1889
   The Philadelphia Inquirer, December 18, 1889.

Anstett dismissed the closed-door theory that was being put forward as the sole piece of evidence to support the suicide theory. He told *The Star* that Gowen never locked his door and that there would have been no reason to lock it if he intended to commit suicide. And if he had committed suicide he would have shot himself in the forehead or mouth and not in the ear.

His argument about the locked door was based on several lines of reasoning.

First of all he said that the last time anyone saw Gowen alive, which was at 3:30 PM the previous day, the bedroom door was not locked. At that time a maid who wanted to clean the room had opened the door and talked to Gowen, who appeared to be working on some papers at his desk. Anstett said that neither he nor any other guest ever locked their rooms, and he was certain Gowen never locked his door.[14]

So, what would have prevented a murderer from walking into the room after the maid had gone away, shot Gowen and then made his escape out the fire exit, which was across the corridor from Gowen's room? Anstett said he had only Wormley's word that the door was locked when the body was found.

Anstett went on to say that he was among the prosecution staff at the Molly Maguire trials and he knew well the hatred the Irish in the coal regions had for Gowen. He was convinced that one of them had taken Gowen's life.

Anstett was also critical of the way Gowen's body had been hurried out of the hotel. He said this prevented anyone from getting to the bottom of what had happened. He also said that James Wormley, who was African-American, was superstitious about having a dead body lying around because he thought it would bring bad luck to his business. So he got rid of the body as quickly as possible.

[14] *The Star*, December 16, 1889

Anstett presented his theories to the police, but since he could offer no evidence on whether or not room 57 was locked when the body was discovered, the police had nothing to act on.

The weakness of Anstett's argument was that it implied a conspiracy, not only by James Wormley, but also by his maid, who claimed that the door was locked at 4:30 PM on Friday when she went back a third time to check the room. This conspiracy would also seem to have involved the head porter and Police Officer Cross, all of whom claimed to find the door locked the following afternoon.

Other Scenarios

A review of *The Star* material indicates that while the suicide verdict presented by the reporter was a plausible scenario that was based on an interview with James Wormley and an hour spent at the death scene, it certainly was not the only plausible scenario that could have been presented based on the available evidence.

If a review of the evidence had taken place by someone other than a newspaper reporter in a hurry to get a scoop out onto the streets of Washington, there were numerous other pieces of evidence in the room that should have been examined in detail -- all of which could have led an investigator to seriously question the suicide theory.

The most obvious of these clues was the second exit from the suite -- the bathroom to corridor exit -- which was not mentioned in the first edition of *The Star* and was only touched on briefly in the second edition. This exit should have been the focus of any serious investigation, but instead it was practically ignored.[15]

[15] *The Star.* December 14, 1889.

In the argument that he said eliminated all possible exits from the room, the reporter described the bathroom door lock as a "snap lock" -- the type of lock, like a Yale lock, that is often found in the front doors of residences and that require a key to open from the outside, but which can be opened from the inside by simply turning a knob. Locks of this type are still in use in older homes across the country even today.

The possibility that the bathroom door provided an easy escape for a murderer was overlooked by the reporter who knew about it, and not focused on at all by the newspapers that were basing their coverage of Gowen's death in *The Star* account. The result was that this important piece of evidence which should have created questions about the suicide verdict from the very beginning was largely ignored.

How important was this second exit? Its importance was that it offered a second scenario -- very similar to Anstett's theory -- for Gowen's death, and this scenario was as follows: a murderer came into the room after the maid had gone away for the second time and shot Gowen in the head. He locked the bedroom door to delay the discovery of the body, and then cautiously opened the bathroom door leading out to the corridor.

Having determined no one was in the corridor, the murderer pulled the nib down, closed the door quietly and walked across the corridor to the fire exit and escaped.

How plausible was this scenario? It was just as plausible as the suicide theory, and the effect of this scenario was to seriously undermine the suicide theory as the only scenario possible that was in line with "the facts" as seen by Wormley and *The Star* reporter.

The possibility of exiting through the bathroom door was not the only issue connected with this bathroom door that was ignored by *The Star* reporter.

Wormley had stated that the key to the bathroom door was in the hotel office, so why did Wormley not take that key for the bathroom door from the office when he was informed that Gowen's bedroom door was locked from the inside, and open the bathroom door and enter the suite, instead of having a staff member climb through the transom into the bedroom?

Wormley had ignored the easy way into the Gowen suite and took the more difficult way of entering through the transom.

There is no record of anyone questioning him about why he did this.

Finally, another question: why did Wormley call in Patrolman Cross to accompany him to Room 57 even before he discovered Gowen's dead body?

A possible explanation is that he wanted an official witness who could testify that all doors were locked when the body was discovered.

Which raises yet another question: how did he know there was going to be a dead body there?

*

THE FAMILY REACTS

While the removal of the body was taking place, Wormley said he sent a telegram off to Francis Innes Gowen, Franklin Gowen's nephew and law firm partner, notifying him of his uncle's suicide. And he sent a note by messenger to Postmaster General Wanamaker, a close friend of Franklin Gowen's, informing him of Gowen's death.[16]

Within a very short time the news swept around Washington, including into Congress, that Franklin B. Gowen had taken his own life. The news created a sensation, and within a short time crowds of people had descended on the Wormley Hotel wanting to know the details surrounding Gowen's death.[17]

Among the hundreds who arrived were Congressmen Maish and Reilly, and Senators Cameron and Quay, all of Pennsylvania, as well as several other members of the New York and Pennsylvania delegations.

Maish and Reilly, who were personal friends of Gowen arrived at the Wormley at 4 PM, and when they discovered that the body had been moved to the police station, they went there to find out the police version of what had happened to Gowen. When they arrived at the station they were horrified to see Gowen's body lying on the floor in a back room and being treated with a complete lack of respect, as members of the public were being allowed in to see the body. The two congressmen called in a local undertaker and had the body moved to the undertaker's establishment.[18]

In Philadelphia, George Delaney, Gowen's private secretary, said he was the first to read James Thompson Wormley's telegram that brought the news of Gowen's death to the Gowen law office in the Forrest Building.

[16] *The Philadelphia Inquirer,* December 15, 1889.
[17] *The Miners' Journal,* December 15, 1889.
[18]*The Philadelphia Inquirer,* December 15, 1889.

Delaney told reporters that he was deeply shocked by the news, because he could not imagine the circumstances that would lead to Franklin Gowen taking his own life. He said such an act was totally out of character for Gowen.

Delaney said he read the communication from the Wormley Hotel several times and hesitated before he brought the telegram to the attention of Francis I. Gowen.[19]

The younger Gowen later said he was stunned by the news.

"I was in my office in conference with my partner when the telegram was received. I thought it was a joke. I sent off a telegram to Washington to confirm the news." [20]

When this confirmation arrived thirty minutes later he sent a telegram to Gowen's wife and daughter at the Gowen family residence, informing them of Gowen's suicide.

Mrs. Gowen said later that she received the telegram from two total strangers who arrived at her door. She was probably referring to messengers from Western Union who delivered the telegram from Francis Innes Gowen.

It is not known how warm the relationship was between Francis Innes Gowen and his aunt, but it seems unusual that a member of the Gowen family was not entrusted to bring this news of Gowen's death to the widow. She was obviously still upset about it the next day when she was quoted in the newspapers about the incident.[21]

Both Mrs. Gowen and her daughter refused to belief that Gowen had committed suicide, and insisted that he must have been murdered by the Molly Maguires.

[19] *The Philadelphia Inquirer.* December 15, 1889.
[20] Ibid.
[21] Ibid.

Mrs. Gowen said that her husband was getting threatening letters from Molly Maguires almost every day, and that one of those Mollys must have killed him.[22]

Other members of the Gowen family had a similar reaction to the news. Parker Hood, Gowen's nephew, told the press that the idea that his uncle had committed suicide was ridiculous.[23]

Parker Hood claimed that Gowen had been in excellent spirits before he left for Washington, and he did not have a reason in the world for taking his own life. He also said he had received information from Washington that his uncle had been murdered.[24]

Mrs. V. Lansdale, a sister of the dead man, refused to accept the news until her husband came home. When her husband met her at the Mt Airy railroad station and confirmed the news that Gowen was dead, she collapsed and had to be assisted to her carriage. But Lansdale, too, said he did not believe Gowen had committed suicide, because he thought that his brother-in-law had no reason to take his own life.[25]

Dr. Charles Darrach, the family physician, stated that he did not believe that Gowen had taken his own life.

"A thought of killing myself could not surprise me any more than this," Darrach said. "Mr. Gowen used to stop in here once in a while when overworked and in need of a little toning up and to get medical advice.

"I considered myself their family physician and I would have been called in case of any need for Mr.Gowen."[26]

[22] *The Philadelphia Inquirer, December* 15, 1889.
[23] Ibid
[24] Ibid
[25] Ibid
[26] Ibid

"He was a man who regularly called on medical science and would not neglect any threatening ailment." Darrach said. "But he was of splendid constitution and temperament and rarely needed anything. I had no idea he was not in perfect health."

As the news swept around Philadelphia, the Gowen law office was besieged with friends and reporters, all trying to find out the reason for Franklin Gowen's suicide. But Francis Innes Gowen could provide no answers. He said Gowen's death was a complete mystery to him.

Pandemonium was also created in the offices of the Reading Railroad, where Franklin Gowen still had many friends and admirers. [27]

Indeed, many of Gowen's old friends were convinced that he would not have committed suicide because he was close to regaining the presidency of the Reading and that he had been looking forward to the appointment. Talk of a Molly Maguire assassination was widespread at the Reading.

After the initial horror experienced by the news from Washington, Mrs. Gowen and her daughter made plans to go to Washington to take possession of the body.

The pair had even boarded the train and got as far as Wayne Junction when Francis Innes Gowen boarded the train and persuaded the two women to return home.

Francis Gowen did not make public any reason why he thought it unwise for Franklin Gowen's wife and daughter to go Washington at that time.[28]

Meanwhile, Francis Gowen was making his own plans to go to Washington, accompanied by his uncle, James Hood, who was also a partner in the Gowen law firm.

[27] *The Philadelphia Inquirer*, December 15, 1889.
[28] Ibid.

Hood and Francis Gowen left Philadelphia on the 5:40 PM train in the company of Robert Linden, the manager of the Pinkerton Detective Agency office in Philadelphia, who had been retained by Francis Innes Gowen to investigate the cause of Gowen's death. Bringing Linden on board seemed a clear indication that the family was unwilling to believe that Gowen had taken his own life and they were convinced that the famous Pinkerton detective would get at the truth.

Linden had a long business relationship with Franklin B Gowen going back to 1875, when Gowen, as President of the Reading Railroad, hired the Pinkerton Detective Agency to identify and bring before the courts a group of Irish mine workers, known as the Molly Maguires, who were, according to Gowen, sabotaging his mines and his railroad and committing acts of murder against his mine bosses.

Linden had been brought on board by the Pinkertons as a supervisor at a critical phase of Gowen's campaign against the Mollys, and it was he who stage-managed the arrest, trials and execution of the Mollys, earning the eternal gratitude and admiration of Franklin Gowen.[29]

It was little wonder, therefore, that Francis Innes Gowen turned to Linden, when the rumor circulated in Washington that Franklin Gowen had been murdered by the Molly Maguires.

His trust in Linden's investigative abilities may have been misplaced, however, because even though Linden had numerous management skills, and he was an expert at generating favorable public relations for the Pinkerton Agency, he did not have the basic skills of a professional detective.

[29] Pinkerton, Allan. *The Molly Maguires and the Detectives.*

Linden's activities on behalf of Gowen in the coal region had involved managing undercover detectives, and he had also displayed a great deal of expertise at manipulating the press. In addition he had perfected a technique of intimidating defense witnesses and getting them to become witnesses for the prosecution. But the ordinary skills of a private detective were absent from his resume, and these were the skills that would be needed to crack the Gowen case.

SHOCK IN PHILADELPHIA

While Linden and Gowen's nephews were on their way to Washington the death of Gowen became the sole topic of conversation in the Philadelphia private clubs where the social elite gathered in the evenings to fraternize before going home to their families.

The *Philadelphia Inquirer* summed up the mood in these clubs in an item on the front page that evening:

GOWEN'S FRIENDS GREATLY SHOCKED

They Decline To Believe That the Famous Lawyer Committed Suicide

The intelligence of the tragic death of Franklin B. Gowen, at Washington, was received with the greatest possible surprise in this city. Mr. Gowen's many warm friends in railroad, financial and legal circles were shocked beyond expression and most of them refused to believe that the death was the result of suicide. The theories of murder and accident were general, and those who believed in the suicide theory were hopelessly in the minority. Those who knew Mr. Gowen best declared it was out of the question for him to take his own life. They said a man of his fine mental abilities, robust constitution and rugged manhood could not have committed suicide. [30]

Effington B. Morris, president of Girard Trust, a leading Philadelphia financial institution and a close personal friend of Gowen's, rushed to the Gowen residence when he heard the news. He told a reporter for the *Inquirer* afterwards that the relatives did not believe for an instant that Gowen had committed suicide. And neither did he.[31]

[30] *The Philadelphia Inquirer*, December 15, 1889.
[31] Ibid.

Morris said that rumors that Gowen was despondent over the way his case was going before the Interstate Commerce Commission was pure nonsense. He said he had never known Gowen to be depressed by a setback, but always bounded back full of energy.

Morris said he could not conceive of Gowen having a gun in his possession, either, because he had never owned one. But above all he could not believe that this man, who everybody knew was devoted to his wife and daughter, would leave them in such a manner.

Morris was echoed by another Gowen friend who said that Gowen was the bravest man he knew and he would have faced up to any problems he might have had and not taken "a coward's way" of solving problems by committing suicide.

Butthere were those who accepted the *Star* verdict because it was alleged that his body was found in a room that had been locked from the inside, with the gun that was supposed to have fired the fatal shot by his side.

Those who accepted this verdict speculated about possible reasons for the suicide. Rumors abounded that Gowen was close to bankruptcy and could not face life as a pauper; that he was distraught over having not been able to win back the presidency of the Reading Railroad, a position that he cherished more than anything else; and that he was consumed with guilt over his responsibility for sending twenty Irish mine workers to the gallows.[32]

Postmaster General Wanamaker disputed the bankruptcy rumor saying Gowen was worth over $300,000, and another friend put his net worth at $500,000. So, the rumor that Gowen was bankrupt was discredited almost as soon as it went into circulation.[33]

[32] *The Washington Star*, December 16, 1889.
[33] *The Philadelphia Inquirer*, December 15, 1889.

The rumor that he was distraught over not being able to regain the presidency of the Reading was dismissed by a number of his intimate friends. It was the consensus of their opinion that Gowen was confident that he would be back at the helm of the Reading and that it was only a question of time when this was going to happen.

Gowen's confidence in his ability to regain control of the Reading was not shared by some of his fellow financiers who stated that it was his mismanagement of the Reading that had put it in such dire straits in the first place. John Hutchinson, a Philadelphia financier who said he was a life long friend of Gowen's, said Gowen took a Napoleonic view of his destiny and he believed that he could never make a mistake in business matters. This led him to monumental blunders, which caused financial ruin to many of those who bought into his schemes. It was the view of Hutchinson and a number of other business associates of Gowen that he would never regain control of the Reading no matter how much he was convinced that he would.[34]

Some of those who knew Gowen well, including Robert Linden, dismissed the theory that Gowen might have committed suicide over the execution of the Molly Maguires. They said it was out of the question. Linden said Gowen was very proud of his part in the Molly Maguire episodes and he was satisfied that the twenty executed men deserved their fate.

Hutchinson said that he had gone with Gowen to the Kehoe trial and Gowen had expressed great satisfaction at the death sentence handed down to Kehoe. [35]

[34] *The Philadelphia Inquirer,* December 15, 1889.
[35] Ibid.

Hutchinson also said that Gowen marched around the streets of Pottsville after Kehoe was sentenced to death and displayed no fear of the hundreds of Irish who filled the streets of Pottsville who were angry at the verdict. Hutchinson tried to persuade him to leave Pottsville as soon as possible, but he refused to go.[36]

"I came here to teach people to respect the lives of others. I see no reason why I should run away," Gowen said.

Hutchinson did not mention it but Gowen probably had some comfort level in knowing he was surrounded by scores of armed Pinkertons. These Pinkertons were under the direct supervision of Captain Robert Linden, who provided a human barricade against those Kehoe friends who might be tempted to get some measure of revenge against Gowen.

As Francis I. Gowen, James Hood and Robert Linden journeyed down to Washington on the evening train to claim Gowen's body, the speculation continued in Philadelphia about the reason for Gowen's death. The vast majority believed that he had been shot by the relatives of the executed Molly Maguires, and if not by a member of this group then by a bankrupt businessman who had been ruined by Gowen, or someone who had a deep personal grudge against him. Indeed, the list of possible suspects was a long one, since Gowen had made numerous enemies during his career.

[36] *The Philadelphia Inquirer,* December 15, 1889.

GOWEN'S LAST DAYS

The rumor mill was running at full production in Washington also when Linden, Francis Innes Gowen and Hood arrived, turning out a variety of spins on Gowen's death. *The Star* had already published a second edition, which featured the Gowen story prominently, giving all the details known about his last days in the Capital.

According to the newspaper, Gowen had spent the morning and afternoon of Thursday, December 12, at the Interstate Commerce Commission arguing a complaint lodged by his client, George Rice, an Ohio oil refiner, against the Rockefeller interests. The complaint alleged that the Rice company was a victim of price fixing by the defendants who were determined to make it too expensive for him to ship his oil to market. If the defendants had been successful in their plot, Rice claimed he would have been forced to sell out to the Rockefeller interests, who, it was charged, were plotting to create a monopoly in the oil business.

It was ironic that Gowen was complaining about a company trying to corner a given market, since he had spent the greater part of his career at the Reading trying to monopolize all aspects of the coal industry. [37]

By the time Gowen had finished his testimony on Thursday he thought the commission was not very receptive to his arguments and he was not sure how the Commission would render its verdict when it handed down a decision the following week. But Rice said he seemed in the best of humor when he parted with him in the early afternoon as Gowen walked back to the Wormley Hotel.

Rice said that Gowen told him that he might return to Philadelphia the following day if he received a telegram about a case pending in the coal regions of Pennsylvania. [38]

[37] Schlegel, *The Ruler of the Reading.*
[38] *The Star,* December 14, 1889.

On the way back to the hotel Gowen met Major Stevens, an old friend, and both went into the Riggs Hotel to join other business acquaintances.

Gowen's conversation with his friends involved speculation about stock market prices. As usual, all of those present were interested in learning about what Gowen thought of a number of stocks, and whether it would be advisable to invest in those stocks at that time.

In spite of his failures in business, Gowen's opinion on the value of stocks was always listened to carefully, mainly because he could make such a convincing argument to back up any recommendation.

After spending a considerable amount of time with his friends, Gowen returned to the Wormley Hotel and was not seen by any of the hotel staff for the rest of the day.

The following day, Friday, December 13, George Rice stopped by the hotel at 1 PM and talked to Gowen for forty-five minutes. Rice said that Gowen appeared to be in a good mood and was not at all disturbed by how the case was going. Gowen had been working at a table covered with documents when Rice arrived, and Rice said he had seemed to be deeply engrossed in whatever he was doing.

Rice said Gowen told him he would see him the following week and that they could only hope for the best about the outcome of the case. Rice then left the room and he did not see Gowen alive again.

At 2 PM Gowen went down to the hotel diningroom and had a substantial lunch. The staff later said that he seemed in the best of humor and had enjoyed a small bottle of wine with his meal. Gowen also engaged many of the other guests in the diningroom in conversation.[25]

[25] *The Miners' Journal*, December 15, 1889.

The only other contact the hotel staff had with Gowen while he was alive was the contact by the maid who had talked to him twice in the afternoon, at 2:30 PM and 3:30 PM as she tried to gain access to the room to make the bed.[26]

*

Shock was the most common reaction to Gowen's death among those in Washington who knew him There was as an unwillingness to believe that Gowen had committed suicide. But the fact that Gowen had been discovered in a room that was locked from the inside and a gun lay by his side seemed a powerful argument to many that Gowen had taken his own life.[27]

Patterson, the Washington Coroner, stated late in the afternoon that he was convinced Gowen had taken his own life and that there was no need to have an autopsy. He based his opinions on interviews with the hotel staff and with the members of the police who were first on the scene. He also viewed the body lying in a back room of the police station.[28]

Patterson had been put in a very embarrassing position by the way the death scene had been handled.

First of all, the owner of the hotel had removed the body from the room before Patterson had an opportunity to view it.

Next, he had ripped up the carpet and had taken the wallpaper off the wall, thus effectively destroying any evidence that might have been in the room. And in the final analysis, Patterson had only Wormley's word for it that the main piece of evidence pointing to a suicide -- a key that locked the door from the inside -- had been in the lock when Wormley said he first became aware on Saturday morning that something was wrong in room 57.

[26] *The Star.* December 14, 1889.
[27] Ibid
[28] Ibid

The police had not helped matters by taking their time about informing Patterson about Gowen's death: Gowen's body had been at the police station for hours before Patterson arrived on the scene.

The police defended themselves by saying that it was four hours before anyone could find Patterson, who seemed to have been out of town early in the day.[29]

However, one result of the way Gowen's body had been handled was the introduction of new laws in Washington regarding crime scenes -- laws that mandated that a body should not be removed from a crime scene, or no crime scene be disturbed in any way, until the coroner first arrived on the scene and gave his approval.

This insured that there be some law and order involved in future crime scenes in Washington but it was too late to do anything about the chaos in Room 57 of the Wormley Hotel.[30]

In spite of his embarrassment about having no control over the initial investigation into Gowen's death, Patterson seemed to have decided to make the best of a bad situation by agreeing with the conclusions made by the owner of the hotel and the police supervisors at the New Jersey Avenue station: namely -- that Gowen had taken his own life.[31]

This verdict seemed to be supported late on Saturday afternoon when it was reported in a second edition of *The Star* that an employee of neighborhood gun dealer, D.N.Wolford, Inc, which was located at 477 Pennsylvania Avenue, came forward and said that a man who bore a resemblance to Gowen bought a 38 caliber Smith & Wesson pistol the previous evening, Friday, December 13, between 7 PM and 8 PM.[32]

[29] *The Star*, December, 14, 1889.
[30] Ibid
[31] Ibid
[32] Ibid

The gun store employee, a man named Smoot, was shown the pistol that had been found in Gowen's room, and he identified the gun as the gun he had sold the previous evening.

The Miners' Journal carried a story on Monday, December 16, about the Smoot identification of the gun and his claim that the man who purchased the gun bore a resemblance to Franklin B. Gowen.

The Washington police now advanced the theory that Gowen had suffered a bout of temporary insanity and left his hotel room shortly after 7 PM and purchased the gun.

He then went back to the hotel and took his own life between 8 PM and 9 PM. The timing of the suicide was determined by the fact that none of the guests in the rooms adjacent to Gowen's room had heard a gunshot, and the only explanation for this was that Gowen had killed himself during the period when the guests were in the diningroom for dinner -- between 7 PM and 9 PM.[33]

No witnesses came forward, however, to say they had seen Gowen leave or return to the hotel on Friday evening.

The police theory about how Gowen met his end seemed like a very reasonable theory to all those who heard of it, and as the evening wore on the tide of public opinion, which had earlier been convinced that Gowen had been murdered by the Molly Maguires, began to drift toward the suicide theory.

But even though this scenario for a suicide seemed to satisfy many observers in Washington in the hours immediately after Gowen's body was found, there were those who believed they had equally good reasons for believing that Gowen had been murdered, and they were very vocal about their convictions.

[33] *The Star,* December 14, 1889.

Those who subscribed to a murder theory based their opinion on one piece of evidence -- the statement made by Wormley and Patrolman Cross -- that when Wormley, Patrolman Cross and the hotel clerk had entered the bedroom in that morning the gas light in the room was off. [34]

The unlit lamp was of primary importance because the cornerstone of the suicide theory had Gowen stand in front of the mirror and put the gun to his head at approximately 8 PM on a December evening. This was three and a half hours after sunset in a room that was almost in complete darkness because the blinds were down and the drapes drawn. Because of the darkened room, it was believed that it would have been completely impossible for Gowen to have seen himself in the mirror, and therefore impossible for him to have guided the pistol to deliver the fatal wound.

The murder theorists argued that it was obvious that a murderer had entered the room shortly after the maid spoke to Gowen at 3:30 PM, when Gowen was still alive and the door was not locked from the inside, and after killing Gowen left the room and escaped down the back stairs. Those who subscribed to this theory argued that the light was not lit at this time because it was still daylight and a light was not needed.[35].

Taken at face value, this seems like a very persuasive argument and many were convinced by it. But there was a problem with this argument also, and again the source of this problem lies in the detailed sketch of the room provided by *The Star* reporter who accompanied the sketch with a detailed description of every item in the room.[36]

[34] *The Star*, December 15, 1889
[35] *The Star,* December 18, 1889
[36] Ibid

According to the *Star* reporter, the blinds on the windows were closed and the drapes were drawn almost shut and given this fact it would seem that there would have been very little light in the room even in daylight.

So, if a murderer had entered the room while Gowen was sitting at the table reading and writing, the light must have been on because Gowen would have needed the light to read and write, and Gowen probably knocked the gas light over when he was shot, and it was the murderer who shut the light off to prevent a fire.

Why would Gowen have the drapes drawn in the middle of the day and the gas light on? No answer has been provided for that.

But a murder taking place in the afternoon poses another problem. If the killer had fired a shot at Gowen's head, or even fired more than one shot at him, why had no one on the floor heard the shots? Gowen's next door neighbor often complained of noise coming from Gowen's room, and since he was in his room that day, why had he not heard the shots? Or why had the cleaning staff not heard the noise? A possible answer is that the killer used some kind of muffling device, such as a coat or pillow.

Nor has there been any focus on another item in the *Star* article, namely that the bed did not seem to have been slept in when the room was opened on Saturday morning -- just a little rumpled. If Gowen was killed on Friday afternoon or evening this would explain why the bed was not slept in on Friday night.

But if the bed had this undisturbed look before Gowen was killed on Friday, then this would mean he had not slept in the bed on Thursday night either, because the maid said she did not get a chance to make the bed.

So, where was Gowen on Thursday night? Was he out? Or did he sit up all night?

It is obvious, therefore, that both competing theories had problems: the suicide theory had the unlit lamp, the dark room, and the second exit; the murder theory had the door locked on the inside and the silence of the gunshots.

Both problems had to be solved before any credible solution to Gowen's death could be found.

THE FAMILY ARRIVES

Suicide and murder theories were swirling around Washington as Captain Linden, James Hood, and Francis Gowen arrived on the evening train from Philadelphia.

The trio had few comments to make to reporters who met them at the railroad station -- they just stated that the reason for Gowen's death would be the subject of an investigation, but at this point in time they had no information on the circumstances invol- ved in the death of Gowen.[37]

On the possibility that the Molly Maguires were involved in his death, Linden said he had already assigned twelve of the best men from the Philadelphia office to investigate any Molly connection. He said they were already on their way into the coal regions.[38]

Linden said that he was aware that Gowen had received many threats over the years from Molly relatives who were bitter over the men who were executed and the number of men jailed. He said the relatives of these men were convinced that Gowen and the Pinkertons had used the legal system in Pennsylvania to set up and murder their relatives.[39]

Linden said, however, he and Gowen had always believed the Mollys were cold blooded killers who had nothing to do with the labor struggle, but were a cult who killed for no other reason than they enjoyed killing. This had been the Pinkerton point of view since the Molly executions and they had been successful in convincing the majority of the American public, right up to the time of Gowen's death, that Gowen had done America a great service by destroying the organization.[40]

[37] *The Star,* December 16, 1889.
[38] Ibid
[39] *The Star,* December 15, 1889
[40] *The Miners' Journal,* December 15, 1889

Linden said he had little doubt that many of the Molly relatives were delighted that Gowen was dead. It was rumored in Washington that when word got out in the coal regions of Pennsylvania about Gowen's death the news was the cause of many celebrations.

But Linden went on to say that only an investigation would determine whether the remnants of the Mollys were involved, and he had every intention of finding out the truth of the matter in due course.[41]

Linden, Hood, and Francis Innes Gowen headed for the Wormley Hotel as soon as they left the train station, and when they arrived they spent an hour with James Wormley in Room 57, hearing his account of how Franklin Gowen had met his end.[42]

They had nothing to say to reporters after they left the hotel, but a member of the hotel staff said Linden had focused on the light being switched off, as this was a possible indication of murder.

According to this source Linden had said that Gowen needed the light to kill himself, and he could not have possibly switched off the light after he shot himself in the head. So, Linden questioned all of the hotel staff who were there when the room was opened, and members of the staff said they were certain the light was not on in the room at that time.[43]

Linden and Gowen's relatives then headed off to the New Jersey Avenue police station to talk to the police who had investigated Gowen's death. The trio also intended to make arrangements to take Gowen's body back to Philadelphia.

[41] *The Star,* December 15, 1889

[42] Ibid.

[43] Ibid.

The scene at the police station early in the day must have been very upsetting for Gowen's relatives when they heard about it, because Gowen's body had been treated with an obvious lack of respect. Gowen's body had lain on the floor of a backroom completely exposed to those who wanted to come in and taken a look at the fallen financier, and there was a continuous stream of people coming in to look at the body.[44]

Unrestricted viewing of the body was being permitted until Gowen's friends insisted that the body be placed in the hands of a private undertaker, who removed it from the premises.

The lack of respect shown for Gowen's body was in marked contrast to the esteem in which he had been held while he was alive. Here was the body of a man who was invited to functions at the White House and who mixed in the top social circles in Philadelphia, Washington and New York. Not only that, but also members of his extended family had married into some of the wealthiest families in the United States.

But after his death his body had received no more respect than if it was that of a vagrant dragged in from one of the back alleys in the city.

The disrespectful treatment of Gowen's body would have been understandable if Gowen had been a criminal. Criminals were often executed in public during this period and their bodies were sometimes left hanging at the gallows for a full day so the public could be entertained by the spectacle.

The bodies of bank robbers killed during a shoot-out with the police were treated with an equal lack of respect and were frequently roped to a door and propped up outside of police stations so the public could see the bloody end of men that the public often thought of as Robin Hood type characters.

[44] *The Star.* December 15, 1889

Linden examined Gowen's blood-stained coat and shirt, and examined the blood stained pistol that the police had given to him.

Then he interviewed Patrolman Cross and his superior, Lieutenant Moore, about their understanding of how Gowen had met his death. Linden listened to everything they had to say without making any comment.

Afterwards, Linden refused to give reporters any idea of what he thought of the evidence unearthed up to that point, saying only that the investigation was only beginning.[45]

Francis Gowen sent for an undertaker named Speare and told him to prepare the body for removal to Philadelphia. When asked if there was going to be an autopsy, he said there would be none; he said that the body would go back to Philadelphia that night for burial.

Reporters asked Francis Innes Gowen about the status of the police investigation into Franklin Gowen's death, and he replied that the investigation was being placed in the hands of Captain Linden, who would have complete control of the matter.

And in answer to a question on what conclusion he had come to on his uncle's death, he said he could think of no reason why his uncle would have taken his own life, and he expected that Robert Linden would get to the bottom of the matter. Francis Innes Gowen then refused to take any more questions from the press. He said that all questions about his uncle's death from that point onwards should be directed at Captain Linden.

Francis Gowen then left the building with Linden and the undertakers.[46]

[45] *The Star,* December 16, 1889.

[46] Ibid.

Those familiar with law enforcement practices in modern times may think it very unusual that Francis Gowen could hand over the investigation of a possible murder to a private investigator. But that practice was not unusual in the late nineteenth century.

Although the coroner had already stated that no foul play was involved in Gowen's death, there were officials in Washington, such as Assistant District Attorney Ker, who said that he did not believe that Gowen had committed suicide and were very disturbed at this rush to characterize the cause of Gowen's death.[47]

The reasons for the uneasiness of some members of the police were numerous. For instance, they had reservations because the suicide theory was based on one single piece of evidence: the key on the inside of Gowen's bedroom door, which was being offered as proof that a killer could not have exited the room, and, therefore, Gowen had to have committed suicide. The police noted that they had only hotel owner James Wormley's word that the key was in this position, and the police would have liked to see more supporting evidence before arriving at any conclusion, or at least an in depth investigation of Wormley himself.

There was also a great deal of resentment in official police circles that this high profile case was being snatched from them and given to the Pinkertons, who had a reputation of circumventing the law when they thought the situation called for it.

The Pinkertons had a reputation back then of being union busters and bounty hunters and their expertise was thought to be in their ability to place informers deep within trade unions, not in the ordinary type of detective work that would be used in investigating Gowen's death.[48]

[47] *The Philadelphia Inquirer,* December 18, 1889.
[48] Friedman, Morris. *The Pinkerton Labor Spy.*

There were those who were even questioning the gunsmith's allegation that the man who purchased the gun on the previous evening looked like Gowen, since the gunsmith first said he thought that Judge Montgomery had purchased the weapon.

Then there was the way Wormley had disturbed the crime scene immediately after the body was removed from the room. By doing this, some police officials believed that Wormley had destroyed any possibility of an objective examination of the forensic evidence when he pulled off the wallpaper and pulled up the carpet.

Wormley's actions were not necessarily viewed by the police as evidence that he was covering up foul play, but those actions made officials like Assistant District Attorney Ker unhappy with the way the Gowen case was being handled by Coroner Patterson.

It would be many years before there were firm guidelines in place throughout the United States about the procedures that were to be followed when a body was discovered and there was a suspicion that foul play was involved. These procedures would be developed over a time span measured in decades and would gradually be adapted all over the country.

But in 1889 Francis Innes Gowen was at liberty to remove the body from Washington and justify it on the basis that Coroner Patterson had stated that he did not intend to conduct an autopsy.

And there was no law on the books at that time that stated that only the police could conduct a murder investigation, so Francis Innes Gowen was at liberty to turn the matter over to Robert J. Linden.

In 1889 Captain Robert Linden had a Jekyl and Hyde reputation that was based on his years waging war on trade unions and other groups considered enemies of capitalists.

Two years later, in 1891 when he was appointed Chief of Detectives of the City of Philadelphia Police Department, his appointment was greeted with widespread opposition from labor unions and members of the working class, who called him a bounty hunter and union buster who would not hesitate to commit murder if it suited his goals.

The establishment on the other hand was completely in support of Linden's appointment because it viewed him as a tough policeman who knew how to keep the lower elements in line.

Linden's poor reputation among the working class was based not only on the agency's tough treatment of the Molly Maguires, but on other anti-labor activities the Pinkertons had been involved in over the years. There was a widespread conviction that the Pinkertons operated outside the law entirely and were just as murderous as the men they hunted down and killed.[49]

This attitude was based in part on the fact that the Pinkertons allowed members of outlaw gangs who had been captured by the Pinkertons to be taken out of jails by vigilante mobs and lynched -- mobs that many believed had been organized by the Pinkertons themselves.[50]

Linden himself was involved in this type of activity in 1875, when Allan Pinkerton ordered him to organize a vigilante group to murder suspected Mollys who were in a violent confrontation with the Franklin Gowen interests.

In a letter written by Allan Pinkerton, which is part of the Library of Congress Pinkerton Papers, Pinkerton ordered George Bangs, his Superintendent, to get Linden to organize vigilantes and to keep Franklin Gowen appraised of Linden's activities.[51]

[49] Broehl, Wayne. *The Molly Maguires.*
[50] Ibid.
[51] The Library of Congress Pinkerton Papers.

Gowen not only had agents like McParland and Linden in the area building up a case against the Irish labor agitators, but when the time came to try the Mollys, he had company lawyers act as prosecutors; the juries were selected from panels of jurors hostile to the Irish; the judges involved were cronies of the coal barons; and the hangmen were brought into the area by the coal barons to insure that the local sheriffs did not botch the hanging of twenty men. All that was supplied by the state was the jail and the ropes.[52]

So, Francis Innes Gowen's decision to set Linden loose on the Molly Maguires was an echo from the past, and his decision to ignore the Washington Police was not without precedent. It was the way law enforcement was often administered in the United States in the late nineteenth century.

[52] Lavelle, John. *The Hard Coal Docket.*

JAMES THOMPSON WORMLEY

James Thompson Wormley, owner of the Wormley Hotel, had a flourishing business, and he enjoyed immense esteem in Washington, since the cream of Washington Society attended functions in his establishment and even presidents patronized his hotel on special occasions.[55]

But on the 14th of December, 1889, a famous American was found dead in one of his suites and there was a debate going on all over the city about whether Gowen had taken his own life or had been murdered.

Worse than that, there was the insinuation by men like Cassius Anstett, a long time hotel resident, that Wormley was part of a conspiracy to cover up a murder committed by the Molly Maguires -- an insinuation that had been already published in several newspapers.

The Wormley Hotel was one of Washington's most popular hotels, and the Wormley Family who owned the hotel had a huge stake in maintaining the hotel's image as one of the most prestigious addresses in Washington.

The Wormley Hotel, located at the corner of Fifteen and H Streets, was popular for a number of reasons. First of all it had the reputation of serving the best food in Washington -- a reputation it had first acquired thanks to the efforts of James Wormley Senior, an African American who had founded the hotel.. Wormley had been a noted chef in the Metropolitan Club and as a private chef to the American Ambassador to London before he opened his own restaurant at the Wormley Hotel in 1871. The hotel also acquired a reputation for its facilities, which were known to be among the best in Washington, and was one of the first hotels in the United States to feature a public telephone.

[55] *The Washington Star.* October 21, 1934

When James Wormley Sr. died in 1883, his funeral was a major event that was attended by some of the most prominent personalities in Washington. [56]

The hotel then passed into the hands of his son, James Thompson Wormley, who had been the first graduate of the School of Pharmacy at Howard University. The family was to be associated with Howard University for generations.

Although several members of the family were physicians and were prominent socially, their race was frequently mentioned in press coverage of the hotel.

Some newsmen, who seemed to believe that they were paying the Wormleys a compliment, mentioned that the family had some "Indian blood," while others noted they had never been slaves, and still others mentioned that there was English blood in the family.

This patronizing coverage in the press must have been very offensive to a family who were achievers by any standard that might have been used to measure their accomplishments. Very few families in the Washington area had such a considerable number of family members who had made a name for themselves in a variety of fields.

But it must have brought home to them that no matter how much they achieved, when a case like Gowen's death emerged, the family was viewed with suspicion and badly concealed contempt, and at the end of the day they were viewed by many whites, even those who professed to admire them, as being members of an inferior race of people.

This must have been a bitter pill to swallow for the aristocratic James Thompson Worlmey -- if he had done nothing to merit this treatment.

[56] *The Washington Star.* October 21, 1934.
   Journal of Negro History, April 1935, Jan. 1936.
   James Wormley Recognition Project, The Agribusiness Council[Wash.]

Because of this attitude, the Wormley knew that he occupied a very precarious position in a society that was completely dominated by a white race who had a negative attitude toward blacks, and who were only patronizing the Wormley Hotel because it provided excellent services. Given that, the death of a very prominent white in the hotel must have been a matter of grave concern.

On the issue of the removal of the body from the hotel, James Wormley had tried to defend himself by saying that it was the police who took the body of Gowen out of the hotel.

But this was not well received since it was widely believed that it was James Wormley who had insisted the police bring the body to the police station. And the police were no help to Wormley because in their account they claimed the removal was Wormley's idea.

There was no official condemnation of the way Wormley handled Gowen's death, although a number of Pennsylvania members of Congress expressed their anger openly at the way the hotel had handled Gowen's body.[57]

However, on Monday, December 16, the Chief of Police of Washington issued an executive order that the scene of a violent death was never to be disturbed or the body removed until the coroner's office had visited the scene and given permission to remove the body.[58]

Thus, James Wormley's actions inadvertently ushered in a new era of police investigative procedures in Washington that would eventually evolve into the sophisticated scientific procedures that are brought to bear on crime scenes today.

[57] *The Star,* December 14, 1889.
[58] Ibid.

Although no public outcry resulted from James Wormley's handling of the Gowen crime scene, there was a widespread conviction that he had contributed heavily to the controversy about Gowen's death that erupted in the days that followed.

In response to criticism Wormley insisted that he had not broken any law, and in that he was correct -- there was no law on the books to cover this situation.

But James Wormley could hardly plead that he saw no harm in the actions that he had taken, because he was a highly intelligent man, and he may have been the only person in Washington who did not see that he had created a serious problem by his actions.

In spite of this, Wormley's account of Gowen's movements in the twenty-four hour period before his death was accepted by Linden and Patterson and eventually by the majority of the residents of Washington D.C. His word also was taken that the bedroom door was locked from the inside -- the key piece of evidence used to promote the suicide theory.

In this modern era, Wormley himself would have been included among the suspects if the death of Gowen was viewed as murder. But there is no indication that the police, the coroner, or Linden considered him a suspect, in spite of the very unusual nature of his behavior.

Wormley may very well have thought that the body would have been the sole focus of any investigation and the scene itself would have been of little interest once the body was removed from the scene.

Certainly in that day and age there was no obsession with forensics, ballistics, and DNA that there is today, and Wormley may have thought it just a good business practice to prepare the room for the next occupant without being aware of the consequences.

However, regardless of how innocent his actions may have been, they were viewed with a great deal of suspicion by many influential people in Washington, who thought there was an ulterior motive in disturbing the crime scene before either the family or the coroner arrived.

JOURNEY HOME

Gowen's body left Washington at 11:30 PM in a special train of the Baltimore and Ohio Railroad. The train consisted of an engine, a combination car and a special luxury car called the Palace Car. Francis Innes Gowen and James Hood were the only passengers. Gowen had arrived in Washington on Monday a successful lawyer and a niche high up in society; now his body was going home surrounded by a storm of controversy. It was an abrupt and unbelievable end to a colorful life.[59]

The Gowen family had made it clear that the wake and funeral of Franklin Gowen was going to be a private affair, and even though they were aware that there were many who wanted to express condolences in person, only the immediate family and a few life-long friends were allowed to call on the Gowen family or attend the funeral services.[60]

The Philadelphia Inquirer, on December 16, described the arrival of Gowen's body back to his home with all the solemnity appropriate for a deceased king. This article not only reflected Gowen's high social status in Philadelphia, but the incredible way that he had departed this life. The following are excerpts from the article, which is rich in imagery.

An intense hush has fallen upon Mt. Airy and all its inhabitants when the beautiful home of Franklin Gowen was visited yesterday. Every twig and blade of grass in the stillness of wintry death were wrapped in a white shroud of death. Commanding all the landscape of Mt. Airy stood the dark, red-topped mansion of the coming dead. Facing this, as though speaking in silence from a quarter of a mile away, stood the little church where he had worshipped.

[59] *The Philadelphia Inquirer,* December 15, 1889.
[60] Ibid.

The tombstones of the Ivy Cemetery shone dimly over the hilltop and through the trees. In the oppressive silence reigning over the place, every one [the inhabitants of Mt Airy] conversed only in subdued tones. They could see as every person had old and young who lived there had seen a thousand times, the form of a noble looking man [Gowen] alight from the train, walk up the boardwalk along the railroad, up another walk leading three-quarters of a mile away to his home. The boardwalk was built expressly for him. He was always seen to walk that way, but the whistle of a strange engine at an unusual hour, 8.12 AM, startled everyone from their contemplation.

ARRIVAL OF THE BODY

The approach of the special Baltimore and Ohio Railroad cars from Washington, the black hearse in waiting, the small group of relatives assembled at the station, were not seen by anyone outside the family, yet all the people there knew what was taking place.

As the hearse bearing the heroic form of Franklin B. Gowen moved up over the bridge and around the graceful curve of Sprague Street, the trees, growing warmer under the outbreaking sunshine, melted drops by thousands all the way.

Only Gowen's brother-in-law Edward V. Lansdale was at the Mount Airy Station, Philadelphia, when the private train from Washington pulled in, and he joined James Hood and Francis Gowen to supervise the unloading of the coffin onto a hearse for the short trip to the Gowen home several hundred yards away on Frankford Avenue.

While the hearse and the undertaker's staff made its way to the Gowen home, the trio then took a short cut across the fields to the house to await the arrival of the hearse.

Lansdale, Hood and Francis Gowen accompanied the body into the parlor, where the coffin was opened to allow Lansdale to view the body. The Washington undertakers had dressed the body in a black coat, black trousers, a turndown collar and a black tie. The lid of the coffin was then replaced and the coffin was placed on a table.

Neither Mrs. Gowen nor her daughter came out to view the body, but remained in seclusion in other rooms in the house. The pair had been in seclusion since they received the news of Gowen's death and had drawn the drapes on all the lower windows of their home.[61]

Up in the Gowen family church, Sunday services were held as usual, but the pews normally occupied by the Gowen family were empty. This was the first time this had happened in living memory, but everyone present knew the reason for it.

Pastor Hill read a brief prayer for Franklin Gowen during the service, a prayer which asked God's compassion for him, without mentioning him by name.

O merciful God and Heavenly Father, who has taught us in Thy Holy Word that Thou dost not willingly afflict or grieve the children of men, look with pity, we beseech Thee, upon the sorrows of Thy servant, for whom our prayers are desired. In Thy wisdom Thou has seen fit to visit him with trouble and to bring distress upon him. Remember him, oh Lord, in Thy mercy; sanctify Thy fatherly correction to him, endure his soul with patience under his affliction and with resignation to Thy blessed will; comfort him with the sense of Thy goodness and lift up Thy countenance upon him and give him peace through Jesus Christ our Lord, amen.[62]

[61] *The Philadelphia Inquirer,* December 16, 1889.

[62] Ibid.

The small congregation departed the church after the service without looking in the direction of the Gowen home, or discussing his tragic end.

There were a few visitors to the house during the day, but these were close friends who were expected to call. However, members of the Hood and Lansdale families met them and they had no contact with Mrs. Gowen or her daughter.

Dr. Charles Darrach, Gowen's physician and his closest personal friend, arrived at noon but did not see the widow or her daughter. Neither did the Rev. S. C. Hill, Gowen's pastor, who arrived later.

Later on in the day, relatives and friends reported conflicting views about the cause of Gowen's death.

It was reported that Mrs. Gowen still believed her husband had been murdered, while Lansdale, who was married to Gowen's sister, said he now thought it possible Gowen committed suicide, while of unsound mind.[63]

Sunday passed quietly in the Gowen household with little traffic either in or out of the house. As evening approached the drapes were still drawn on all windows of the house, and later on the lights in the house were extinguished one by one.

[63] *The Philadelphia Inquirer,* December 16, 1889.

A QUESTION ABOUT STRATEGY

Robert Linden did not make an appearance at the Gowen household when the body arrived on Sunday, December 15th. Nor had he been on the special train that had brought the body back to Philadelphia. Instead he told reporters on Monday that he had busied himself supervising the twelve special agents who had fanned out across the coal regions to investigate a possible Molly Maguire connection to Gowen's death.[64]

Although twelve agents seemed like a considerable amount of manpower to assign to this project, when one considers the vast number of possible suspects involved who lived in widely separated areas, it would be a miracle indeed if the Pinkerton agents came up with anything useful, unless they were prepared to drag the investigation out for months, or even years.

A long drawn out investigation would not be acceptable to the Gowens, however, who seemed to want answers immediately.

Franklin Gowen had frequently stated that he had received death threats from embittered Mollys, but he had never filed a complaint against anyone, nor had he given the name of anyone who had threatened him. It must be assumed, therefore, that these threats were anonymous, so the Pinkertons would have little to go on except the knowledge that there were hundreds -- or maybe thousands -- of people in the coal regions who would have loved to see Gowen dead.[65]

But when Linden talked to reporters on Sunday afternoon, he made a remark that should have seemed peculiar to those who had an in-depth knowledge of the Molly Maguire episodes.

[64] *The Star,* December 16, 1889.
[65] *The Philadelphia Inquirer.* December 16, 1889.

Linden said he was targeting those Mollys who had been released from jail in recent years as prime suspects, because they were probably the bitterest enemies Gowen had.[66]

This statement was peculiar for two reasons. First of all, while it was very likely that the released Mollys were bitter enemies of Gowen, their animosity would not have been nearly as intense as the relatives of the twenty men who had been executed. These relatives hated Gowen with a passion because they believed he had murdered their loved ones.

According to Linden, McParland and other Pinkerton agents who had infiltrated the Mollys during the 1870s, another reason was that any Molly with a grudge against a mine boss or other person never got revenge by his own hand -- he always got a person who was a total stranger to the victim to carry out the punishment. This insured that there were never any witnesses who could lead the police to the instigator of the killing.[67]

James McParland and Linden had both testified to this practice during the Molly murder trials, which had taken place across the coal regions, and given the publicity that this practice received in the national newspapers it should have been well known to that section of the public who had followed the Molly saga in the press.[68]

If Linden's and McParland's testimony in the Molly trials was an accurate reflection of the way the Mollys went about the business of revenge, then why would Linden target the person with a grudge for an investigation instead of targeting some of their friends or relatives? Why the change in strategy?

[66] *The Philadelphia Inquirer*, December 18, 1889.

[67] A. Pinkerton. *The Mollie Maguires and the Detectives.*

[68] Ibid.

Nevertheless, the result of this change in strategy gave Linden a very short list of suspects to investigate, which may have been the reason he changed the strategy in the first place. The number of Molly Maguires released from prison could have numbered no more than a dozen, and this was a number of suspects that could be easily handled by his twelve Pinkerton agents.

JAMES WORMLEY SENIOR

ROBERT J. LINDEN

JAMES McPARLAN

ALEC CAMPBELL

FRANKLIN B. GOWEN

ALLAN PINKERTON

ROOM 57 -- The Wormley Hotel

BATHROOM

< Window |===========| Bathroom Exit >
                      Bath

                                        Door to Bedroom
                                      ....[   ] ----
          Bureau
          =======
          * Blood

< Window   Door To Corridor >

            *Gun
  < Fireplace   ++++++++   Table and Chair
               Body | ======= |

                                    * Lamp
  < Window

                                              Bed
                                          | ==== |

  Heavy Wardrobe
Covering double-door entrance to room 56

THE WOUND

While Linden was in Philadelphia supposedly keeping in touch by phone and telegram with his agents in the field, a new controversy erupted in Washington over a report in *The Evening Star*, which stated that unnamed sources in the Washington Police Department claimed that the nature of the wound in Gowen's head made it impossible for him to have shot himself.

These sources said that Gowen could not possibly have committed suicide because he could not have held a gun near his head at such an angle that the bullet would go into the skull behind and above the right ear and come out in the middle of the left ear.

Furthermore, it was being argued, that the absence of any burn marks around the wound -- the entry wound was clean-- was proof that the gun must have been held three or four feet away from the head. These sources argued that this made it impossible for the wound to be self-inflicted.[69]

Coroner Patterson was infuriated by this fresh controversy and he met with the press to deal with the issue of why there was no burn marks at the entrance wound. He said that when a pistol is held tightly against the flesh all the burning powder goes right into the wound, leaving the outside rim of the wound free of burn marks or smoke marks.[70]

It was, therefore, obvious, said Patterson, that Gowen had held the gun tightly against his skull and the result was the absence of burn marks. Patterson went on to say that he wished the newspapers would leave the investigating of Gowen's death to professionals whose skills lay in this area, and not go rushing into print with every theory presented by those with no expertise in this area.

[69] *The Star* December 17, 1889.

[70] Ibid.

There were several problems with Patterson's response to *The Star* story. First of all he failed to respond to the issue that a person could not shoot himself in the head from this angle.

Secondly, his explanation of why there was no burn marks around the wound suggested that this coroner had little experience with gunshot wounds, because the police were making legitimate points, not only with the absence of burn marks at the entrance wound, but with the angle at which the bullet had entered the skull.

On the issue of the angle: the angle required to send a bullet into the skull at a point an inch behind and above the right ear and exit through the middle of the left ear would require that the gun would have to have been held at such an angle that it would be almost impossible to get a finger anywhere near the trigger. A simple experiment with a toy gun confirms this.

This gives rise to another question: even if Gowen managed to get the gun in the position necessary to achieve this result, why would a man bent on killing himself make the chore so extremely difficult by pointing the gun at his head in this bizarre angle, and in doing so also run the risk of only wounding himself seriously, or worse, still, leave himself brain damaged and paralyzed, not able to talk or walk, but very much aware of the hopeless condition that he was in.

The coroner's explanation for the absence of burn marks at the entrance wound also defied common sense and was disputed by a member of the Washington police who had some expertise in this subject. He argued that the barrel of a gun becomes extremely hot after a bullet is fired, and this is especially true of the muzzle of the pistol that would burn when touched, so it defies reason to suggest that a gun pressed tightly against the head would produce no burn marks. On the contrary, there should be a neat little red circle at the entrance wound that should be clearly visible, as well as some tattooing around the circle.

The coroner's rebuke to reporters to stop printing opinions about a subject that they were not qualified to answer also ignores the fact that the unnamed reporter was only quoting a third source: an unnamed police supervisor.

But, the following day *The Star* quoted an army surgeon brought to them by Patterson, who Patterson claimed confirmed his diagnosis of the bullet wound.

However, the surgeon's statement was so ambiguous that it could be interpreted in any number of ways.

The following is the statement issued by the army surgeon:

If the pistol were placed in contact with the skull before the discharge there would be no blackening of the flesh around the wound of entrance as it would all enter the wound. If the pistol were held at a distance from a few inches up to several feet, as would naturally be the case with a suicide, there would probably be a considerable portion of the flesh marked by the scattering powder. This, however, is not invariably the case and the absence of all blackening and of the mark made by the smut of the pistol when held in actual contact would not prove beyond all doubt that the pistol was held at more than arm's length from the body at the moment of discharge. Moreover, the extent and nature of the blackened portion depends largely on the kind and size of the weapon, on the nature of the powder, whether quick or slow burning, smokeless or otherwise, or the amount of powder used, or the relative weight of the powder and the ball and also on the character of the flesh in the immediate neighborhood of the wound so that it is next to impossible to lay down any invariable rule in the matter. It will be remembered that in the case of Mr. Gowen there was no smut mark found or any space blackened by the burnt powder.[71]

[71] *The Star,* December 18, 1889.

Coroner Patterson used the army surgeon's statement to support his theory that the gun was held tightly to the side of the head, but the surgeon clearly stated in his final statement that it was "next to impossible" to come to any firm conclusion on the matter. The surgeon was also focusing on burn marks caused by powder and not on the burn caused by the red-hot muzzle, which would have caused a burn mark when placed against the head.

In the final analysis Patterson was in no position to claim to have knowledge about how Gowen used the gun, since he was not present when the gun was fired.

The police sources would not let it rest however. A source claimed that there was a study done during a murder trial in Pennsylvania twelve years previously, and the study involved firing bullets into a corpse with the gun being fired at various distances from the flesh: from four feet out; from three feet out; from two feet out; from one foot out; and finally with the gun pressed up against the flesh. The gun pressed against the flesh produced burn marks, but no smoke marks or tattooing of the flesh; the gun fired from other distances produced varying degrees of smoke and grime marks; the bullet fired from the furthermost distance left smoke on the face but a clean entrance wound.

As if this did not provide enough problems for the coroner's interpretation of the significance of the wound, a Doctor Porter, who was a resident of the hotel and apparently saw the body before it was removed, came forward to inform the *Philadelphia Inquirer* what he saw in Room 57 on the morning of December 14.

The Inquirer described Porter's description of Gowen's body in the following manner:

The body was lying on its back with a bullet hole about two inches above and back of the right ear, the brains protruding and a mass of blood congealed in the left ear. Powder and smoke begrimed the right side of the face.

The presence of smoke and grime marks suggested that the bullet had been fired from some distance of several feet and not fired when the gun was pressed against the head, which put Patterson and Porter on a collision course.

Patterson did not respond to Porter's comments in the *Philadelphia Inquirer*, and none of the other major newspapers picked up on the item at all.

Nor did the other national newspapers pick up on the police argument that because of the angle of the bullet's trajectory, the wound could not have been self inflicted, and *The Star* did not follow up on the story, either, so Patterson was under no pressure to respond to the issue in the days that followed.

The result of this was that *The Star* account published on December 14 remained a major source of information on what happened to Franklin Gowen on the day he died. But the wound became a key issue that was responsible for keeping the controversy boiling over on how Gowen had really met his death.

The police had the last say in the matter. On Monday, December 16, a police source cited statistics that indicated that the vast majority of self inflicted wounds were in the temple or the mouth and not in the side of the head.

So while the hullabaloo over the wound continued, it remained to be seen how Linden would handle this, once he began to focus on the case.

THE LINDEN INVESTIGATION BEGINS

With a mandate from Francis Innes Gowen to conduct the investigation into Gowen's death and a clear indication from the wife and daughter of Franklin Gowen that they believed Gowen had been murdered, Captain Robert Linden arrived back in Washington on Monday morning, December 16, to continue the investigation into Gowen's death.

The Molly Maguires were prime suspects, but Linden knew well that there were scores of other people out there who had suffered grievously because of Gowen's business practices and any one of them could have been angry enough to kill him.

Then, there could have been enemies of Gowen that the family or his peers knew nothing about, such as jilted lovers or an acquaintance who had been betrayed or ruined by Gowen.

If Gowen had been found dead in 2002 instead of 1889, the police would have carefully interviewed all those who knew Gowen in an attempt to ferret out a motive for his murder, and the investigation would have been long and painstaking.

When Linden arrived back in Washington on Monday, he said he was going to devote all his energy to unearthing the reason for Gowen's death, and the assumption could be made that he would leave no stone unturned until he uncovered the truth.

There were a number of problems that were generating controversy and it was assumed Linden would focus on them once he began to work on the case. Among the issues was the unlit lamp in the bedroom, and the failure of anyone in the hotel to hear the gunshot.

Then there was the dispute over the burn marks on the entrance wound, and a dispute over the distance of the gun from Gowen's head when the gun was fired.

However, there was one item that was missing from the controversy and this was the fact that it was possible to exit from the bedroom through the bathroom door leading to the corridor. No one, including the police, seemed to focus on this issue.

Linden had little to say to the press since Saturday evening when he announced that he had his agents out investigating the Molly Maguires to find out if the Mollys were involved in the murder. But by Monday afternoon he was dropping hints on the way his investigation was going, and these hints did not indicate that his entire focus was on the Molly Maguires.

Instead he told reporters he was investigating all possibilities, including murder, accidental death, and suicide while suffering from temporary insanity.[72]

Linden's position was a little unusual to say the least. He had been hired to investigate a murder, but here he was in the early hours of the investigation entertaining the idea of accidental death or suicide while of unsound mind.

Some reporters viewed these remarks as an indication that Linden was backing away from a murder theory and moving toward a suicide theory that would be compatible with the Coroner's verdict.

But, if this was so, on what grounds was Linden moving to the suicide theory, if indeed he was? Was he, like Patterson and Wormley, satisfied that the locked door constituted proof of suicide, and that all other issues were irrelevant? Or did he have another reason he was not revealing to the newspapers?

Some reporters theorized that the temporary insanity theory and the accidental death theory were being brought up by Linden in order to ease the pain of the family in case his investigation concluded that the Mollys had nothing to do with Gowen's death.

[72] *The Philadelphia Inquirer,* December 18, 1889.

But even if the Mollys were found innocent of any involvement in Gowen's death, why end the investigation there? Why not open a new phase of the murder investigation? There were a score of people who had been deeply wounded by Gowen, and all of them should have merited some kind of investigation.

It was understandable that Linden might bring up the temporary insanity theory because Christians who had a suicide in the family could not bear to think that a loved one had abandoned them to the shame of suicide while in full possession of his faculties. Not only did a suicide bring a terrible social stigma to the survivors, it was also viewed by most Christian sects as a mortal sin that resulted in eternal damnation for all those who committed suicide while in a sound state of mind.

Thus, it was thought that Linden was promoting the Gowen family piece of mind by bringing up the insanity theory -- although the family was still left with a suicide, which was a stigma no matter what the reason for it.

Linden also tried to plant the idea that Gowen might have accidentally shot himself while examining the gun, but this theory was met with widespread rejection because the angle the bullet entered the head made it virtually impossible for a gun to be discharged accidentally.[73]

As Linden continued his investigation he said there were a number of issues that were the subject of dispute and that needed to be clarified before any final decision could be made on whether Gowen's death was a murder or a suicide.

First, there was the issue of who had bought the gun. There were conflicting views circulating because the gun dealer was not totally positive about who had purchased the pistol.

[73] *The Philadelphia Inquirer,* December 18, 1889

Linden decided to clear the matter up by going to the gun dealer with the gun in his possession. Lieutenant Moore of the Washington police department accompanied him.

Since a man named Smoot, the clerk at the gun shop, had already come into the police station on Saturday and identified the gun as the one he had sold personally to Franklin Gowen on Friday evening at approximately 8 PM, it could be assumed that Linden just wanted to confirm Smoot's identification.

The following is Smoot's account of the sale of the gun, which he gave to the police early on Saturday evening. This account was published in the *Miners' Journal* on Sunday, December 16:

Smoot, the young man who sold Gowen the pistol and cartridges with which he killed himself, says he paid no special attention to his customer or his purchase. It [the sale] *was a common occurrence and he would never have given it a second thought if he not read in the newspapers of Gowen using the same kind of gun to kill himself. Then it occurred to him that it might have been the very same pistol that he had sold, and he notified the police of the occurrence. He identified the pistol in their possession brought from Gowen's room by Patrolman Cross as the one he had sold on Friday to the elderly gentleman, answering the description of Gowen. Smoot's statement is important as not only establishing the fact that Gowen had committed suicide, but as fixing the time of the suicide. Smoot states that the transaction he described took place between 7 and 8 o'clock on Friday evening.*

Based on Smoot's statement, the police had come to the conclusion that Gowen had left his room between 7 PM and 8 PM on Friday evening, while suffering from a bout of temporary insanity, ... bought the gun ... and then went back to his room and used the gun to kill himself.

This was a logical assumption, but there was a problem: the light in the room was off when Gowen was found, so how could he shoot himself in the dark.

When Linden and Moore arrived at the gun shop Moore had with him a woodcut of Gowen's likeness that was clipped from a Washington newspaper, but instead of meeting with Smoot, who does not appear to have been present during Linden's visit, Linden met with Walford, the owner of the store. When the meeting was over, Walford met with reporters and told them he not only identified Gowen as the man he personally had sold the gun to, but he had made a mistake on naming Friday evening as the day he had sold Gowen the weapon -- that Gowen had purchased the weapon on Thursday evening.[74]

Walford also said that his son was in the store with him when the gun was purchased, and both thought at first that the man who bought the gun was Judge Montgomery, but they decided later that it was Gowen.

Walford made no mention about the identification made by his clerk at the police station or of the statement the clerk made about being alone in the store when the gun was purchased.

Since Moore was one of the police officials who had interviewed Smoot on Saturday and it was on the basis of this interview that the press were informed that Gowen had bought the gun, the question arises about why Moore did not challenge Walford's version of who had sold the gun to Franklin Gowen.

This was not a minor issue in the investigation into the death of Franklin Gowen, indeed it was a major issue, because it focused on whether Gowen had bought the gun, and if, in fact the gun purchased at Walford's was the death weapon. Yet we have two separate accounts of the purchase of the gun, and though Linden and the police were aware of the discrepancies, there was nothing published in the newspapers that they tried to sort out these discrepancies.

[74] *The Star*, December 18, 1889.

Walford's announcement about being confused about the date of the purchase was a surprising development. On Saturday, Smoot was emphatic that the purchase was made the previous night, but now the owner comes along on Monday and says it was sold on Thursday night, and he was the one who sold it.

This would prove to be a very significant development.

In his conversation with reporters, Walford said that Linden had come into his store and looked around for some time before identifying himself. Walford said Linden then questioned him on the purchase of the gun and asked him to check his records on the actual date of purchase. It was at this point he said that he discovered he had given the wrong date initially.

Why had Linden asked the dealer to check his records? What grounds did he have for believing that the initial report that Gowen had bought the gun on Friday might not be accurate?

Linden then produced a Smith & Wesson and asked Walford if this was the gun purchased by Gowen.

Walford unscrewed the pearl handle of the gun and noted the serial number on the gun and also the fact that blood had seeped in behind the pearl handle. The serial number was the one his records listed for the Gowen gun, which Walford considered proof that this was the murder weapon and that Gowen had purchased it.[75]

Before he left the store Linden said the information supplied by Walford clearly established that Gowen had purchased the gun on Thursday evening, but he asked Walford not to talk to reporters about the subject of their conversation.[76]

However, Walford said he saw no need to obey Linden's instructions, because he did not see any importance in the information that he had provided.

[75] *The Star,* December 18, 1889.

[76] Ibid.

Nevertheless, the information provided by Walford did in fact convince most people in Washington and Philadelphia that Gowen had indeed committed suicide, because in the days, months, and years that followed two pieces of evidence were offered as conclusive proof that Gowen had taken his own life: one was the bedroom door locked from the inside; the other was the blood-stained revolver that Walford said Gowen had purchased from him. To many, it seemed pointless to question the suicide theory any further.

Given Linden's hints earlier in the day that he was considering suicide as an option, one wonders if he had made contact with the gun dealer earlier in the day, hours before his very public visit with Captain Moore, and that he was simply using the gunsmith as a device to let the Gowen family, who only wanted to hear about a murder investigation, know that at the end of the day Linden might hand down a verdict that Gowen had died from a self-inflicted wound.

Walford's "mistake" about the day that the gun was purchased seemed to provide Linden with a solution to a second problem that clouded the suicide verdict from the beginning -- the problem of the light being out when it was thought initially that Gowen had committed suicide between 7 PM and 8 PM on Friday.

The sequence of events presented by the police earlier fitted perfectly except for the light being unlit. The sequence supposedly went as follows: Gowen had a fit of temporary insanity between 7PM and 8 PM on Friday evening and during this mental dis-turbance he went out and purchased the gun from the Walford store.

Gowen then went back and stood in front of the mirror in his bedroom between 8 PM and 9 PM and put the gun to his head and pulled the trigger.[77]

[77]   *The Star*, December 15, 1889.

But the absence of a light in the room was an insurmountable problem for the suicide theory: how could Gowen see his way around a room in the pitch dark never mind stand in front of the mirror to shoot himself when he would not have been able to see himself in the mirror in the first place?

It did not seem possible, and this issue was lending credence to those who argued that someone else had shot Gowen

So, the unlit lamp remained a serious problem, until Walford stated that the gun had been purchased on Thursday evening, not on Friday evening.

The problem it solved was as follows: if the gun was purchased on Thursday evening, Linden could now argue that Gowen had pulled the trigger shortly after the maid had knocked on his door the second time, at 3:30 PM.

When she returned at 4:30 PM, 5:30 PM and 6 PM, the door was locked from the inside and there was no response to her knocks. Because of this, it was assumed by Linden that Gowen was already dead at 4 PM and, furthermore, he had pulled the trigger while there was plenty of light in the room, so there was no need for the light to be on.

This was a credible solution to the problem of the light, but in solving this problem there arose another one: Gowen had obviously not suffered a "brainstorm" between 7 PM and 8 PM on Friday evening which drove him out of his room and into the gun shop to buy a pistol.

So, in solving the light problem, Linden had inadvertently cast a shadow over his temporary insanity theory, although he did not mention this problem and neither did any of the reporters who covered the new timelines in stories published the following day.

Nor did any members of the press focus on the conflicting evidence given by Smoot and Walford, although this conflict should have been the focus of a great deal of attention.

The third problem Linden faced in the early hours of his investigation was the continuing insistence by a few members of the Washington Police that the angle the bullet took through Gowen's skull and the clean nature of the wound precluded anyone inflicting such a wound on himself.

Linden did not even try to get in the middle of this debate, but instead backed up the coroner's position -- that when the gun was pressed tight against the victim's head all the debris exiting the gun barrel went into the wound and the wound remained clean.

The U.S. Army surgeon who had came forward and seemed to voice support for Patterson's theory gave it a great deal of credibility in spite of the fact that his statement seemed to contradict Patterson.

The problem that was posed in accepting Patterson's theory about the wound is that it was not the only scenario in which the wound in Gowen's head would have lacked any burn marks.

For instance, it was claimed by those who believed that Gowen was murdered that the clean wound could have been a result of a murderer firing the bullet from a distance, a theory that can hardly be disputed.

So, the problem of Linden's position was that he was accepting the coroner's theory as the only valid theory when a theory of murder was equally valid, based on the evidence available.

But without other supporting evidence, there was no way of deciding which scenario was correct.

Of the two conflicting theories, the coroner's theory was the weakest, since he had no supporting evidence at all.

Those who believed in the murder theory, on the other hand, pointed out that Dr. Porter, the first doctor on the scene, said Gowen's face was smeared with smoke, which supported the theory that the gun was fired from a distance.

Although Linden must have been aware of Porter's testimony, he continued to support the coroner.

Coroner Patterson and Linden, however, were not always on the same page, and the conflict in their views led to further talk of conspiracies.

About the same time that Linden was moving the time of the suicide back from 9 PM to 4 PM in order to resolve the conflict over the unlit lamp, Patterson had moved the time of the suicide up to 7 AM the following morning to achieve the very same result: resolve the problem of the unlit lamp.

Linden did not confront Patterson on this issue, being satisfied that they agreed on one important issue: the light in the room was not unlit because some murderer shut it off, it was unlit because Gowen did not need a light to kill himself.

Patterson's new timelines for Gowen's suicide set off a debate on how long it takes for rigor mortis to set in. According to Wormley and the police the body was stiff when it was found at noon and since this was only five hours after Patterson believed that death had taken place there was a dispute about whether or not rigor mortis could have taken place in less than eight hours.

When the issue was first raised on Saturday afternoon, Patterson said the body was cold but flexible when he found it, and since this was in direct conflict with Wormley's account, Patterson was accused of meddling with the timelines in order to deal with the problem of the unlit lamp.

Patterson was furious about these charges and gave an angry rebuttal in the *Evening Star.* Quoting Charles Maymott Tidy a British authority on rigor mortis, in a book entitled *Legal Medicine,* Patterson said that in the 92 cases of death that Tidy had examined, rigor mortis occurred in two cases in two hours; in 14 cases in three hours; in 31 cases in four hours; in 14 cases in five hours; in 20 cases in six hours; and 11 cases in seven hours.

As far as Patterson was concerned this was documentation that rebutted those who claimed rigor mortis could not have set in five hours.

However, it did not explain why Patterson initially claimed the body was cold but flexible, implying that rigor mortis had not set in when he viewed the body at 4 PM -- nine hours after he said death had taken place.

This discrepancy would be just one item in a long list of items of evidence that continued to plague the investigation into Gowen's death.

Linden's investigation into when the gun was purchased solved two problems for him but did not put to rest the issue of the wound and a debate would continue on this issue for several days.

In spite of the fact that he seemed successful in putting to rest the issue of who bought the gun and why the light was not lit, Linden inadvertently created two more issues by solving the first two problems.

First, everyone involved with the case had difficulty understanding why no one claimed to have heard a gunshot when Gowen shot himself.

It appeared that the walls were not that thick in the Wormley Hotel and it was thought that the gunshot should have been heard by at least one of the guests, or one of hotel staff who were walking in the corridors.

This was especially mysterious because of the fact that Gowen's room 57, was separated from Room 58, a room permanently occupied by General Shriver, a retired army officer, by sliding doors which were locked in place, but which did not provide an effective sound barrier because the general had on occasion complained about the sound coming from Room 57.[78]

A solution had been found for this mystery initially by arguing that Gowen had killed himself between 8 PM and 9 PM, when all the guests were down at dinner and when all the maids had already gone home for the day.

But when Walford moved the purchase of the gun back to Thursday and Linden moved the time of the suicide back from 9 PM to 4 PM to solve the unlit light problem, the question about why no one had heard the gunshot emerged once more. All the guest were in their rooms at this time, and all the maids were in the hallways, and it certainly seemed reasonable to assume that someone would have heard a shot.

But Linden had no solution for this problem and ignored it throughout the rest of his investigation.

The second problem that emerged from switching the day the gun was purchased involved the actual suicide. In his efforts to let the Gowen Family down easily, Linden had been dropping hints about "temporary insanity" as a reason for Gowen taking his own life This tactic seemed to have been designed to ease the Gowen family into believing that their loved one had absolutely no control over his actions and therefore was not responsible for his own death.

But by unearthing the new evidence that the gun was bought on Thursday night, this raised questions about Gowen's alleged fit of "temporary insanity."

[78] *The Philadelphia Inquirer.* December 18, 1889.

The issue then became a public discussion that posed the question -- how long does a fit of temporary insanity last?

While most people found it credible that Gowen had some kind of "brainstorm" on the evening of Friday, December 13, and in the middle of this attack had gone out and bought a gun, there were many who had great difficulty in believing that he had this alleged brainstorm on Thursday evening ... bought the gun ... and then functioned for the rest of the evening and all day Friday as if nothing was wrong.

How could Gowen argue intelligently before the Interstate Commerce Commission all of Thursday afternoon if his intentions were to go out and buy a gun later in the evening?

How could he chat amiably with his friends in the Riggs Hotel before going to the Walford store to purchase the weapon?

How could he meet with his client Mr. Rice, from Ohio, in his hotel room on Friday at 1 PM and talk intelligently about business if he had self destruction on his mind as soon as Rice left?

How could he have a relaxed lunch between 1:30 PM and 2:30 PM ... be writing at his desk at 3 PM when the maid arrived to make the bed ... and then put a gun to his head shortly afterwards and kill himself, without leaving any written explanation for his actions? Instead, he seemed to have interrupted a brief he was writing. It was this sequence of events that was not easily reconciled with the idea of temporary insanity.

Of course, neither the public nor the medical profession in the late nineteenth century had studied suicide in the way it was studied in the twentieth century.

It is now known that a minority of those who commit suicide give no indication in advance that anything is wrong, and not only that but once they have made a firm decision to go through with the suicide they even become happy and upbeat because they believe that their problems -- whatever they are -- will be solved shortly.

Thus, their suicide may come as a total surprise to those close to them. However, in the majority of cases there are warning signs in advance that all is not well with someone who is considering suicide.

Linden did not acknowledge in public that moving the purchase of the gun from Friday to Thursday had caused any problems with his temporary insanity theory -- he continued to promote the idea until Gowen was buried, without anyone challenging him on the question.

POSSIBLE REASONS FOR SUICIDE

While Linden was in Washington on Monday investigating Gowen's death, opinion in Philadelphia had moved in support of the suicide theory, and theories were being advanced about possible reasons for the suicide. Many of these reasons were provided to reporters by people who were friends of the Gowen family. One rumor that gained a great deal of currency was that Gowen was nearly bankrupt and could not tolerate the humiliation of the public knowing that his fortune was gone.

The basis for this rumor was a story going around that Gowen had borrowed $100,000 from a New Jersey financier named Alfred Sully from Hackettstown and was then unable to pay it back on December 1, the due date. Supposedly, Gowen went to Sully and received an extension of time, until December 7, but when that date came he was still unable to pay and Sully was threatening a law suit.[79]

The Sully story was given credibility because borrowing large sums of money was nothing new for Gowen. In the days after his death some of his wealthy friends told about the huge sums of money he had borrowed -- not all of which were paid back.

John N. Hutchinson, a long-time friend said he had loaned Gowen $200,000 when he got into financial difficulties, but he had been paid back on that occasion, and on other occasions when he had also loaned Gowen money.[80]

But Hutchinson said not everyone had been as lucky as he had been when he or she invested in one of Gowen's schemes, and he knew many people who had lost a great of money by putting their faith in Gowen's ability to pay them back.

[79] *The Philadelphia Inquirer,* December 17, 1889.

[80] Ibid.

"Many people had lost money by following Mr. Gowen's sanguine views as to the advance in the value of the [Reading] stock," Hutchinson said. "The rainbow of promise he saw so clearly was after all only a rainbow, and it was to him a source of sorrow that he had even remotely caused his friends the loss of their money."[81]

Hutchinson went on to say that Gowen was a gambler who had powerful powers of persuasion. He had the ability to convince many people to continue to invest huge sums in Reading stock, even when auditors were publicly saying that Reading stock was highly overpriced.

"Is there any other man who in one day could induce a keen, cunning and cautious capitalist like William H. Vanderbilt to buy over 70,000 shares [valued at $2,000,000] of Reading stock when he might as well have spent the money in a bucket shop?"[82]

There is little doubt that Hutchinson thought that he was paying his deceased friend a great compliment when he told the story of how Gowen had used his powers of persuasion to entice the wily Vanderbilt into investing in what was almost worthless stock. Hutchinson seemed to think Gowen's power of persuasion was a gift from God, but there were many families living in Pennsylvania who had little admiration for Gowen's powers of persuasion, because he had used his talents to destroy them financially, or had, years earlier, run smaller family owned coal and railroad companies into bankruptcy so the Reading could take them over.[83]

These families viewed Gowen with a great deal of bitterness, and, like the relatives of the executed Molly Maguires, thought Gowen a con man who had engaged in criminal activity and got away with it.

[81] *The Philadelphia Inquirer,* December 17, 1889.
[82] Ibid
[83] Ibid.

The story about Gowen's financial difficulties forced Francis Gowen to state that he and James E. Hood had applied for letters of administration for Gowen's estate, and that there was no record of this $100,000 loan.

Francis Gowen went on to say that his uncle's estate was worth $450,000, of which $350,000 was in personal effects and $100,000 in real estate.[84]

Given the value of the estate it would seem Gowen would have no trouble paying the loan, if it had existed.

This put an end to the Sully loan rumor, but created a fresh batch of gossip about what had happened to Gowen's will, which had been known to exist in 1886, but had vanished in the meantime.

Francis Gowen said a search of Gowen's papers on Sunday failed to turn up the will, so on Monday morning, shortly after the Register's office opened, Francis Gowen and James E. Hood, applied for letters of administration, which were granted by Register Gratz. Gowen's widow, Esther B. Gowen and his daughter, Esther Gowen, renounced their claims to administrative function in favor of his law partners.

No explanation was given for the missing will, or for the speed with which the administrative process had begun -- less than forty-eight hours after Gowen's death.

While talk of the missing will entertained some segments of the public, friends of Gowen told reporters why they thought Gowen had committed suicide. The consensus of opinion was that Gowen's faculties had been deteriorating for some time.

[84] *The Philadelphia Inquirer*, December 17, 1889.

One neighbor said that Gowen had, in previous weeks, seemed preoccupied and had a "distant look" in his eyes. Another said that he had missed his stop several times at the Mt Airy station and had to take a train back. Still another, Charles E. Smith, said Gowen was absent for twenty-four hours and was found in the woods, staring into the Wissahicken River.[85]

Then there was talk of a brother who had gone insane and then disappeared, never to be seen again.

All of this talk was offensive to the Gowen family and statements were sent to the newspapers by the Gowens stating that there was no substance to any of these stories about Gowen's mental health: that he was happy and in the best of spirits when he left for Washington on Monday morning.

Then, through a spokesperson, Gowen's wife once again stated that she could not accept that her husband had committed suicide. As far as she was concerned it was totally out of the question. And she continued to believe this in spite of the fact that on Monday Linden was publicly stating it was possible that Gowen had taken his life while suffering a temporary fit of insanity. According to Linden the locked door, the purchase of the gun from Walford, and the blood on the handle of the gun was proof Linden said he found difficult to ignore.[86]

Linden's statements to the press, which confirmed Coroner Patterson's verdict, set up a discussion in the Philadelphia press about whether a person had to be insane to commit suicide. Various authorities on the subject were interviewed and their opinions were published in the newspapers.

[85] *The Philadelphia Inquirer,* December 18, 1889

[86] Ibid.

These discussions were one more public humiliation the Gowens had to endure as they prepared Franklin Gowen for burial.

The *Philadelphia Inquirer* was the first to focus on the subject and the paper rounded up a variety of experts to help it come to a conclusion on the matter.[87]

The *Inquirer* posed a number of questions related to suicide and then requested the experts to respond to them.

The newspaper justified its examination of the subject at that particular time on the grounds that Gowen was a national celebrity and the public had the right to know what drove him to take his own life.

The various views and theories which have recently been advanced in attempting to explain how Franklin B. Gowen was led to take his own life have aroused public interest in questions of this kind. There has been a revival of discussion of the relations between suicide and insanity in medical and other professional circles, and much expressions of opinion from private sources. Hundreds of cases of suicide occur in the community every year, and although some of them shock and horrify the public for the time being the vast majority pass without comment. But here was a man - brilliant, of great importance to the community in his particular sphere, loved and respected by many friends, unharrassed by social, domestic or financial entanglements, or any of the usual motives for suicide - who, in the very midst of his work, and while apparently in the complete possession of his more than usually alert faculties, took his own life. Such a death as this cannot pass without comment. It completely sets aside the ordinary received views of suicide and affords new food for speculation on this subject.

The *Inquirer* then asked Dr Henry Leffmann, a noted expert in this field the following question:

Do you think it possible for a man in full possession of all his faculties to commit suicide?

[87] *The Philadelphia Inquirer*, December 21, 1889.

Leffmann responded by saying that it was possible for a sane man to commit suicide if he was in great pain from an incurable disease, or if he did not want to be captured by the enemy in battle and chose to throw himself out in the open where he will be killed. He said, however, that suicide was viewed by society as either criminal or cowardly and the insanity device was used to spare the feelings of the family.

Another expert, Dr Charles Mills, said sanity and insanity were relative terms, and that a person could have all the appearances of leading a sane, successful life while masking serious mental problems that cause him to drift into periods of insanity. He said that when the patient was sane that suicide was improbable, but in the dark moments anything was possible.

However, Dr William Pancoast said he did not believe a man would take his own life if he was totally sane. He said there had to be hidden deep-seated problems there all along, very often well disguised from friends and relatives. Pancoast believed that it was impossible for a sane man to do away with himself.

These expert opinions did little to solve the riddle of Gowen's alleged suicide, and gave no comfort to the Gowen family.

In the final analysis Gowen had given no hint of mental problems, hidden or otherwise, no financial difficulties, and no reason that was apparent to anyone why he would do away with himself. So, the controversy continued.

Even though the debate over Gowen's mental condition was very public and no consideration was given to the feelings of the Gowen family by the papers, there was one subject that seemed to be off limits to the papers -- the attitude of the Grace Protestant Episcopal Church, of which Gowen was one of the wardens-- toward suicide.

Most of the main Christian churches in the nation, including the Catholic Church and the Episcopal Church, characterized suicide as a mortal sin, and, according to a strict interpretation of the Church guidelines on suicide, those who died in mortal sin would suffer eternal damnation. The only exceptions were if the sinner somehow had regrets before he expired, or, if she or he was not in control of their faculties because they were insane. Then the extreme penalty -- an eternity in Hell-- might not apply.

It was the Church condemnation of suicide as a mortal sin that led many religious families to lean toward the temporary insanity theory as an explanation for the suicide of a loved one. While this would not lessen the pain and the shame of a suicide in the family, it would, at least, not compound the agony by the idea that the loved one had also gone to Hell.

Some members of the Gowen family in the end seemed to accept the theory that Franklin Gowen had committed suicide while insane, even though this seemed little better than believing that he took his own life while in full possession of his faculties.

However, Gowen's wife and daughter refused to accept these theories and insisted in believing he had been murdered, even though the murder theory carried a great deal of baggage also.

The baggage carried by a family victimized by the murder of a family member is complex. For instance there is a tendency by society to blame the victim, as if somehow no victim could be entirely blameless for his or her own murder. If the murder involved a rape... did the victim provoke the sexual attack; if the murder was the result of a robbery, was the victim carrying too much money; if the murder occurred as a result of a quarrel, did the victim provoke the quarrel?

In the Gowen case, there was whispers about retribution for the executions of the Molly Maguires, a theory that was offensive to some members of the family, who found it difficult to accept that the socially inferior Irish Catholics had brought down the aristocratic Franklin Gowen. It was as if the very idea demeaned the memory of the great man. Probably the only scenario that would have been more offensive would be to have Gowen killed by a lover, or over a lover. This would have been most offensive of all.

Even so, Mrs. Gowen was prepared to carry the burden of being a widow of a murder victim because it seemed to her infinitely more preferable than to be the widow of a suicide. A suicide while in the full possession of his faculties could not be accepted at all.

It was unusual, however, that there was no gossip printed in the papers about the possibility that Gowen might have been killed over a bankrupt businessman out to get revenge, or even that his death was the result of a love affair gone wrong.

Those who still believed in the murder theory focused only on the Molly Maguires, and they were willing to be convinced that if the Mollys did not kill Gowen, then his death must have been the result of a suicide.

Even if one makes allowances for differences in the way that murders were investigated more than a hundred years ago and the way that they are investigated in 2002, it still seemed very unusual that only one suspect -- a Molly Maguire -- was ever considered by the Pinkertons, and that just two pieces of evidence -- the door locked from the inside and the gun bought from Walford -- was allowed to be considered proof of Gowen's suicide. All else was ignored.

Today the death of someone like Gowen would have attracted a score of detectives and all evidence would have been put under the microscope.

And the evidence provided by any one individual would not have been accepted as Gospel until this evidence was supported by other witnesses and a great deal more circumstantial evidence.

MRS. ESTHER GOWEN

Mrs. Esther Gowen, the widow of Franklin Gowen, was no stranger to adverse publicity. For much of her married life Franklin Gowen was getting attention in the newspapers; some of it favorable, some of it hostile. But she learned to endure it.

She was still in her early twenties when she met Gowen in Sunbury, Pennsylvania, and was impressed by his ambition and impressed at his unending efforts at self promotion. But she was also made aware early in the marriage that Franklin wanted to succeed at any cost and he was not that concerned about who he injured on his way up.

Gowen was never an astute businessman, although he had convinced himself that he was immensely talented. His first foray into business in the Pottsville area ended in bankruptcy and a $10,000 judgement against his name. But he walked away from this experience blaming his partner for his downfall, even though his lack of expertise was the major cause of his going out of business.[88]

His downfall created some bad publicity, but Gowen was back on his feet after a twelve-month apprenticeship in a law office, and soon he was making $18,000 per year as a lawyer, a tremendous sum in those days.

The Gowens received some favorable publicity when Gowen became one of the leading lights in the cultural life of Schuykill County, earning glowing notices for his performances on stage and attracting large audiences to his poetry readings.[89]

An Anglophile, Gowen was attracted to the works of major British writers and he believed that he was raising the standard of the cultural life of the citizens of Schyukill County when he staged British plays or read the works of leading British poets.

[88] Schlegal, *The Ruler of the Reading.*
[89] Ibid

It was during this period that Mrs. Gowen learned that her husband had the ability to mesmerize audiences and could persuade them to see the world as he saw it. It was a talent he used later in his career to influence juries in the Molly trials, and later on to persuade investors to put their financial resources in the Reading Railroad.

During his years in Pottsville he also revealed that his patriotism had limits. When the draft was introduced to get recruits for the Northern Armies in the American Civil War, Gowen used an option open to the wealthy -- he hired a substitute, which allowed him to avoid the draft, and he stayed at home with his law practice while others his age who were less affluent went off to fight and die on the battlefield.[90]

Gowen's brother served honorably in the army but this did not save Franklin from accusations that he was a coward, all of which had to be endured by Esther Gowen, who kept a low profile to survive the bad publicity.

But it was not until he became the president of the Reading Railroad that Franklin Gowen began to generate massive publicity that continued year after year. The publicity focused on a number of issues.

First of all there were many Reading shareholders who were unhappy with Gowen's rapid expansion of the company into coal mining and coal distribution, as well as his acquisition of smaller railroads which were added to the Reading portfolio.[91]

All of this expansion was financed with borrowed money and inevitably the company had a huge debt, with the interest payments eating up most of the company's profits. There were accusations of dishonesty and conduct bordering on the criminal leveled against him, which must have been hard for Esther Gowen to endure, since she was prominent in Philadelphia social circles.

[90] Schlegal. *The Ruler of the Reading.*
[91] Ibid.

But it was his confrontation with the unions and his war on the Molly Maguires that generated publicity on a national scale and made Gowen a household name throughout the United States.[92]

Not all the publicity generated over the Molly Maguires was unfavorable, however.

Indeed many of the nation's newspapers hailed him as a hero who was combating a gang of dangerous anarchists. But he was an anti-Christ to the union movement and a tyrant comparable to Cromwell to the Irish mine workers, and in the end his mismanagement of the Reading and the continuous confrontations with the unions made him a liability to the stockholders and he was ousted by the English-based owners of the Reading.

Through all these years of turmoil Esther Gowen remained the dutiful wife, supporting him in public and defending him whenever the spotlight was turned on her.

It is not known what she expected of Franklin Gowen in return for her decades of support and her unwavering loyalty, but she hardly expected that her tempestuous life with him would end in this way, with a telegram arriving at the door carried by strangers informing her that he had abandoned her in the worst possible way, by killing himself in his hotel room in Washington.

As might be expected her reaction was shock and an unwillingness to believe the news.

Esther Gowen knew her husband better than anyone and she was absolutely convinced that he could not possibly have taken his own life. She thought an act like that would have been totally alien to him.[93]

[92] Schlegal, *The Ruler of the Reading.*
[93] Ibid.

In the days that followed she had to endure the worst kind of publicity: her family's life was dragged through the pages of the newspapers, with no subject off limits. This was even more humiliating than when her husband was being accused of being a mass murderer over the Molly Maguire episodes.

It has never been made public what Esther Gowen ultimately knew about the circumstances involved in Gowen's death. But whatever she knew she kept to herself and it has not become part of the Gowen family folklore.

CASE CLOSED

Robert Linden arrived back in Philadelphia on Monday evening, December 16, to attend the funeral of Franklin Gowen, which was being held the following day. Linden said he intended to wrap up his involvement in the Gowen case shortly, but in order to do so he had to take care of two loose ends, both of them major. One was the issue of the wound, which continued to generate controversy in both Washington and Philadelphia; the other was his three-day old investigation of a possible Molly Maguire involvement in Gowen's death.

Given the amount of issues that were continuing to be debated, Linden seemed to have conducted a superficial investigation and was rushing helter-skelter toward a conclusion. It must have been difficult for many observers to understand why he was in such a rush to bring closure to the case, since no one appeared to be pressuring him to wind up his investigation.

The major problem that Linden faced in the day prior to Gowen's burial was the continuing controversy over the wound, and he seemed determined to put this issue to rest if at all possible. Some members of the Washington Police continued to express reservations about the coroner's verdict and the issue continued to fester. Linden had not supported the coroner openly on this issue but since the coroner's interpretation of the wound was critical to the suicide theory, Linden had not openly opposed the coroner either.

However, Linden recognized that if he did not calm down the controversy over the wound, then he would not be able to put the murder/suicide controversy to rest, so his strategy as he arrived back in Philadelphia to attend Gowen's wake was to get support for the coroner's verdict, before Gowen's body was assigned to the grave.

Linden himself had a great deal of experience with gunshot wounds during his long career with the Pinkertons, and because of this he may have had reservations about Patterson's theory, in spite of the fact that he appeared to accept that the wound was self-inflicted.

Part of the reason for the coroner's lack of credibility was the fact that no one was in the room when the pistol was fired and, therefore, the coroner could at best give an educated guess on what really happened in the room at the Wormley Hotel.

And since the wound would have had the same clean appearance if the gun were discharged from four feet away, this only added to a general unwillingness to go along with the way Patterson was interpreting the evidence.

Because of this, it was predictable that there would be many who would claim that Patterson could never know for sure what had gone on in Room 57, because he did not see the body at the crime scene and did not see the crime scene before it was disturbed.

Linden was also aware that his own reputation and his take-charge demeanor could only be credible up to a point, and that this was a major issue and it had to be dealt with or it would continue to percolate.

Unlike Patterson, Linden enjoyed a great deal of credibility and could put the wound controversy to rest, if he presented a theory in a credible way. But in order to be credible he had to have information that supported his theory.

During the Molly Maguire episodes, Linden had proved himself a master at manipulating the press. He had carefully cultivated the press during the Molly trials, feeding them sensational information about the Mollys, with the result that the defendants were demonized.

Indeed, Linden was so effective that in the days immediately preceding the Molly executions, he succeeded in getting American newspapers to publish numerous stories that claimed that the Mollys were about to launch all-out attacks on Pottsville and Mauch Chunk if the executions took place. Based on these reports Franklin Gowen and Linden asked the governor of Pennsylvania for the support of State militia units, who then entered the coal region towns to protect its Welsh and German citizens from being massacred by the so-called wild Irish.[94]

But, the reality was that there were no Molly Maguire hordes up in the hills -- they were a fiction created by Linden to insure that the Mollys did not escape the rope. The newspapers did not send reporters up into the hills to see if these Molly hordes existed, but instead went along with the Linden fiction. And even when the hordes failed to materialize, no paper published a story afterwards that questioned the reality of these hordes, because every pronouncement made by Linden was treated as if it were Gospel.

Ever since the Molly Maguire episodes Linden was viewed in some circles as a larger-than-life lawman, like an eastern Wyatt Earp, who had a great deal of credibility and an integrity beyond question.

Of course, there were those in the trade union movement and in the Irish-American community who saw him in an entirely different light and considered him a vicious, dishonest bounty hunter who would lie if the price was right and who only told the truth when he was contradicting himself.

Now, twelve years after the Molly executions Linden hoped that the newspapers would accept his opinions once again without question.

[94] Campbell, *A Molly Maguire Story.*

Linden was worried about the dispute over the wound, and he decided he needed to solve the problem that evening in the Gowen home, and his strategy was to enlist the aid of Dr. Darrach, the Gowen family doctor, but Doctor Darrach proved a reluctant collaborator in the project.

Linden approached Darrach and asked him to examine the bullet wound in Gowen's head to determine whether or not there was any powder marks or burn marks around the entrance to the wound. Darrach was very reluctant to do this but agreed when Linden insisted. The following account of Darrach's examination of the wound appeared in *The Philadelphia Inquirer* on December 18:

No opportunity was offered to friends to see the dead face. The casket was opened but once after it entered the house. Mrs. Gowen under the earnest advice of her friends and physician, refrained from looking at her dead husband. But Dr. Darrach and Captain Linden made an examination of the wound that caused Mr. Gowen's death.

Their object was to satisfy themselves on the one point: whether powder marks had been made on the skin and whether the shot was [fired], therefore, as close [to the head] as it should be in a case of suicide. The casket was opened by Undertaker Kirk. The head was gently turned aside revealing the bullet hole, just on a level with the top of the right ear and behind the ear, just at the upper end of the mastoid process of the ear, and in that common little hollow where if anyone presses his finger he will find it seems to point against the very throne of intelligence. The hair was not shaved off, as it was easy that by parting it to make a critical examination of the skin with a microscope as well as the naked eye. The hair was not singed.

When Darrach examined the wound he could see no tattooing of the flesh, and it should have been there if the gun was held close to the skull. Darrach told Linden that it had been years since he had been involved in a case like this and he had little expertise, but nevertheless he could not see any powder marks on the flesh.

Linden was disappointed but tried to make the best of the situation by telling Darrach that modern [1889] cartridges had powder with very small grains that were not that obvious to the naked eye, and he assured Darrach that the powder marks were on the flesh. Darrach examined the wound again but still could not see them, and he requested a magnifying glass, which he used to look at the wound close up. But again he could see no powder marks.

Afterwards Darrach was asked if he believed Gowen had committed suicide, but he evaded the question by replying "Captain Linden is sure Mr. Gowen committed suicide."

Later Linden tried to enlist the assistance of the undertaker, Mr. Kirk, on the existence of the powder marks, but Kirk said he could not see them either.

Linden then approached Francis I. Gowen and enlisted his testimony, but Gowen replied that he had not seen the wound in his uncle's head in Washington and did not want to look at it now, and was, therefore, in no position to make any comment about the wound.

Francis Gowen's stance on the wound issue raises some questions. When he went to Washington with Linden on Saturday evening to take charge of his uncle's body, he viewed the body in the undertaker's establishment. It seemed odd, therefore, for him to say on Monday that he had not seen the wound.

In any case Linden was the only person who claimed to see powder marks around the wound -- the powder marks that would prove that the gun had been held close to Gowen's head.

But in spite of Linden's effort to convince the Gowens that Franklin Gowen had committed suicide the body went into the grave without this issue being resolved, and it would be one of many issues that would cloud the question of how Franklin Gowen really met his end.

*

Linden's three-day investigation of the Molly Maguires should have raised questions when he announced the results of that investigation late on Monday evening. But it did not. Linden's opinion on the Molly Maguire issue was published in newspapers across the nation the following day.

Linden said he had concluded the investigation and his agents had interviewed all the Molly suspects who had been released from jail recently, and found that none had been in the vicinity of the Wormley Hotel on Friday 13th, 1889. Therefore he concluded that there was no Molly Maguire involvement with Gowen's death.[95]

Linden's investigation should have raised red flags for two reasons: one, he had confined his list of suspects to those who had recently been released from jail; two, his twelve-man team had taken only three days to complete the investigation, a very small amount of time considering the scope of the investigation.

But the national newspapers printed his conclusions without question, and Gowen went to his grave with the Mollys exonerated from having any role in his death.

The Gowen family, who were well aware of the way the Pinkertons operated during the Molly era, made no public comment about the way Linden handled the Molly investigation.

[95] *The Pottsville Republican.* December 20, 1889.

But the issue must be raised: if Linden were serious with his Molly Maguire investigation what plan of action should he have followed? What could have been more productive than going to those who had been released from jail and asked them to give an account of their movements?

For one thing, he could have gone into the Pinkerton files and pulled out the membership lists compiled by James McParland, the undercover Pinkerton agent who infiltrated the AOH, of particular AOH divisions whose members were especially active during the confrontation with Gowen in the 1870s. According to McParland the AOH and the Molly Maguires were one and the same in the coal regions.

He could have made a list of all the names of those who belonged to AOH divisions whose members had gone to the gallows.

If the Molly Maguires had murdered Gowen, those comrades of the executed Molly Maguires who had escaped the rope or avoided jail would probably have carried out the deed. Either that or the crime had been committed by those male relatives of the jailed or executed Mollys who carried a murderous grudge against Gowen.

James McParland could have been an immense help to Linden in his investigation, because who knew more about the AOH divisions in the coal regions than McParland? McParland was manager of the Denver Pinkerton Agency when Gowen was killed and all Linden would have to do is call McParland up and tell him that he had a list of suspects and who did he think might have carried out a murder on their behalf ... and McParland should have been able to provide him with important leads.

Perhaps he did call McParland, but when McParland was interviewed in Denver about Gowen's death he made no mention of the Molly Maguires being suspects or that Linden had contacted him.

All McParland said was that he understood that Gowen may have committed suicide because of his litigation with the Rockefeller interests.[96]

The national newspapers did not report any Pinkerton invest-igation of any particular Molly friends or relatives, and Linden did not volunteer any details on such an investigation.

And without any opposition except from some members of the Gowen family, it was the Linden spin on Gowen's death that went into the history books.

[96] *The Miners' Journal,* December 20, 1889.

THE FUNERAL

Gowen's funeral was a private affair. The family indicated that it had always been Gowen's wish to have his funeral private, but in view of his life-long pursuit of publicity it would seem more likely that probably he would have liked to be buried with the pomp suitable for a king. But the manner in which he died made it imperative that only the family and life-long friends be on hand for the event. Gowen was buried in Mount Airy Cemetery, which was in sight of the Queen Anne House where he had lived.

The citizens of Philadelphia honored the family's wish for privacy, even though the Gowen story was all over the city's newspapers on the day of the funeral. There was little effort made by anyone to view the funeral procession from the house to the graveyard, even from a distance.

The funeral service was held in the livingroom of the Gowen home with only men in attendance in the room. The female relatives sat in a room nearby where they could listen to the services.[96]

The continuing absence of Mrs. Gowen and her daughter from any involvement in the wake was noted in the newspapers but not commented on publicly.

There were a number of possible reasons for the absence of the widow and her daughter. They could have been distraught by Gowen's death and were unable to take part in a final farewell. Or they knew something about the death of Gowen that so disturbed them that they wanted to distance themselves from his body.

In either case, their absence from the wake and funeral was unusual, because traditionally the next of kin played a prominent role in such ceremonies even if they were grief-stricken.

[96] *The Pottsville Republican,* December 18, 1889.
The Philadelphia Inquirer, December 18, 1889.

The presence of the Rev Dr. Furness of the First Unitarian Church was another unusual aspect of the services. It was noted in the newspapers that he was the pastor of the church that Mrs. Esther Gowen attended.

Obviously, Franklin and Esther Gowen honored God in separate churches, which was a practice that was not entirely unheard of, but which indicated that Mrs. Gowen had not followed her husband's lead in all matters.

Among the family groups who attended the service were the Hoods, the Ropers and the Lansdales, who were cousins and in-laws of the Gowens. Among the Gowens were Mrs. Gowen, Esther Gowen, Gowen's daughter, Henry Gowen, his brother, and Francis I. Gowen, his nephew.[97]

Only a dozen close friends had been invited by the family, among them Postmaster General Wanamaker, Edward Ingersoll, LT. Salinac and Eckley B. Coxe. Robert Linden was also present.

Several members of the clergy who were present took part in the funeral services, each contributing to the liturgy. Among these were the Rev. Dr.William H. Furness, the Rev Dr. Samuel C. Hill, and the Rev Dr. Innes. The services included the regular service of the Protestant Episcopal Church, followed by the Thirty-ninth and Ninetieth Psalms, and the lesson, First Corinthians, 15th chapter. [98]

Dr Furness gave a sermon on the mysteries of life and death, and the service was ended with prayers by the Rev. Dr. Hill and the Rev. Dr. Innes. The service was concluded in less than an hour and most of the invited guests departed from the house immediately and did not accompany the body to the graveyard, which was three quarters of a mile away. A procession of thirteen carriages headed for the cemetery in a downpour of rain.

[97] *The Philadelphia Inquirer,* December 20, 1889.
[98] Ibid

Only a few of the men and none of the women accompanied the body to its final resting place: there were no pall bearers and the staff from the funeral home carried the body from the hearse and placed it in the grave.

The committal service at the graveside was read by Rev. Mr. Hill, who departed with the other guests immediately afterwards.

Only Francis I. Gowen remained to watch the last clod being thrown into the grave, and when this was completed he departed in a carriage for his own home, and Gowen's widow and daughter were left alone to endure their grief.

Gowen was buried with his twin sons who died while infants.

After all the mourners left the graveyard a number of residents of the Mt Airy area drifted quietly into the graveyard and went to the Gowen gravesite. Among these were old friends who had known Gowen from church, or had worked for him in the Reading. They came to say goodbye.

THE QUESTIONS CONTINUE

In spite of the fame he enjoyed during his lifetime, when the earth covered his coffin Franklin Gowen's name might not have appeared in American history books were it not for his war on the mine workers union, the Ancient Order of Hibernians, and the Molly Maguires.

Gowen was only one of scores of powerful American financiers who lived during this period and his problems with the Reading Railroad or his controversial death would never have been enough to earn much attention in American history books were it not for his prominent role in the execution of the Molly Maguires.

The Molly Maguires became legends after their executions and their story continued to be told generation after generation, with the memory of the Mollys kept alive by the popular and scholarly books that come on the market from time to time, and since Gowen played the major role in the Molly saga, their immortality insured that his name remains well known, although the Gowen name is rarely mentioned in a laudatory manner.

After the funeral, the press coverage of Gowen was greatly reduced in the newspapers and there were just a few more articles published that focused on the controversy that surrounded his death.

One such article that was published in *The Philadelphia Inquirer* suggested that a Molly Maguire, who was getting revenge for the execution of a friend, had killed Gowen.

The Philadelphia Inquirer ran the item on December 23, 1889, on the front page.

HAD GOWEN A DOUBLE

Startling Clue Furnished by an ex-Mollie Maguire

THE LAWYER FOLLOWED FOR YEARS

A Stranger dressed Like Gowen Said to Have the Revolver, Entered the Hotel Room, Shot His Victim and Then Escaped.

Special to the Inquirer

Wilkes-Barre, Dec. 22. An ex-Lodge Master of the Mollie Maguire organization furnishes a local newspaper with what he claims is a sure clue to the Gowen tragedy. He says the ex-president of the Reading Railroad did not commit suicide, but was murdered by a man who impersonated the lawyer and in appearance resembled him very much.

The man in question had been following him for years with a view to taking his life. In order to carry out the plot successfully the stranger dressed exactly like Gowen, and during the week the lawyer spent in Washington his double noted every movement.

It was he who purchased the weapon at the Washington store. Returning to Wormley's, he watched Mr. Gowen, and when the latter left the hotel the stranger went up to Gowen's room and secreted himself.

When Gowen returned the man in the room threw his overcoat over him and then shot him. The murderer, then with the aid of an assistant, escaped by way of the window. The murderer blamed Gowen for many of the murders in the coal region, and to avenge the death of a friend on the gallows he made up his mind to kill the railroad man sooner or later.

THE FAMILY'S VIEWS CONFIRMED

Mrs. Gowen and the immediate relatives of the deceased lawyer in Philadelphia have from the first positively refused to credit the theory of suicide.

They said the facts of the case were against any such assumption, and were firm in the faith he was murdered.

The statement of the Mollie Maguire confirms in a startling manner the family's views.

*

A second news item that promoted the theory that a Molly Maguire had assassinated Franklin Gowen was published in the *Mauch Chunk Democrat,* Carbon County, Pennsylvania, the following week, on December 28. The item was attributed to another publication, the *Philadelphia Record.*

GOWEN WAS MARKED

If the Mollie Maguires or some of the adherents of this old-time organization did not kill Franklin B. Gowen, it has been conclusively demonstrated during the last few days that they contemplated the murder of the former President of the Reading Railroad Company. In confirmation of reports that the life of the great lawyer was in danger, Rev. J. T. Gray, pastor of the Paul Street Methodist Church, Frankford, said yesterday in reference to the death of Gowen.

" I almost feel that Gowen was the victim of an assassin. One week before his death I was visiting the Wyoming coal regions and a friend(whose name I do not care to mention), who keeps a large store there and supplies miners principally, said to me: "Mr. Gray, the Molly Maguires, I fear, are moving again, and it bodes no good to Mr. Gowen, and I would not be surprised to hear of his assassination at any time. I fear that he is being shadowed wherever he goes. "

Mr. Gray continuing, said: The moment I heard of Mr. Gowen's death I realized how prophetic were the words of my friend in the coal region, and I now fear that Mr. Gowen was really murdered by some enemy who was on his track.

Little attention was paid to the articles published in the *Inquirer* or the *Mauch Chunk Democrat*, both Pennsylvania papers, because by this time most members of the Washington and Philadelphia public had been convinced by Linden that the Mollys had nothing to do with Gowen's death.

Anyway, these stories lacked credibility because they were quoting unnamed sources that claimed an unnamed murderer or murderers had killed Gowen and no evidence was being offered to support these claims.

Even though the articles found a ready audience among those who believed in conspiracies, those who liked to see a little proof before they made up their minds considered the articles too vague even though they found some elements of the articles believable -- like the animosity of the Molly relatives toward Gowen or the possibility that a gunman had entered the room and shot Gowen.

But an article published in the *New York Herald* on December 23 did create an upsurge in interest in Gowen's death in the New York area and gave some credibility to those who were still claiming Gowen had been murdered.

This particular article had credibility because it was based on interviews with two of the major players in the Molly saga, Captain Robert Linden, and Father McDermott, former Catholic pastor in Pottsville during the Molly era, who had been an outspoken critic of the Molly Maguires. The quotes of each of these men suggested that the truth was not being told about Gowen's death.

McDermott had been a bitter foe of the Molly Maguires until the eve of the executions, but then he went public claiming that some of the men about to be executed were innocent.[99]

The following is the article published in the *New York Herald.*

WAS GOWEN MURDERED?

HIS RELATIVES WILL NOT BELIEVE HE COMMITTED SUICIDE

[BY TELEGRAPH TO THE HERALD]

Philadelphia, Dec. 23, 1889. *There seems to be no doubt that relatives of Franklin B. Gowen are, through the Pinkerton Detective Agency, pushed a systematic and searching inquiry into the manner of the Reading ex-president's death. The brother, Henry Gowen, the widow and surviving daughter cannot be convinced that Mr. Gowen committed suicide, and base their opinion on the fact that there is not the slightest evidence to prove he should take his own life.*

It is learned that the whole truth has not been told about the condition of the room in which Mr. Gowen's body was found at Wormley's Hotel in Washington. The windows of the room were not fastened, as given out. On the contrary they were not even shut down when the doors were opened after the tragedy had been discovered.

[99] Campbell. *A Molly Maguire Story.*

Captain Linden admitted this afternoon that this was the case. He at first said he did not care about talking of the case in any way on account of the family and friends.

He was then told that information had been obtained about the windows being up, and the question was put, "is it not true that the windows were unfastened and raised."

"Yes," he replied.

At the same time he reiterated his previously expressed opinion that Franklin B. Gowen committed suicide.

*

The *Herald* reporter then gave an account of his interview with Father McDermott.

Rev. Father McDermott, now pastor of St. Mary's Roman Catholic Church, was stationed in Pottsville during the Mollie Maguire days. He was the spiritual director of the six men who were hanged in that city on June 21, 1877, for the Mollie Maguire murders. Father McDermott was asked today if he had any theory in regard to the death of Mr.Gowen. He replied:

" I believe Linden would say the opposite of what he means in order to turn away public attention in a case that was put in his charge. You know such is the policy of all men placed in Linden's position."

I next asked him if he thought all the Mollie Maguires hanged were guilty. and he replied:

"I cannot answer the question."

Do you think that any ill feeling still exists in the minds of the children or relatives of the men Gowen helped convict?

"I am not prepared to make a statement in that respect. The history of that affair has never been properly written. I shall make a statement one day, and when I do I will come out strong.

McDermott then made a statement that contradicted much of what Linden and Gowen had testified about the Molly Maguires during the Molly trials: *"No such organization as the Molly Maguires ever existed. The only order was the Ancient Order of Hibernians."*

The *Herald* article is of interest for several reasons. First of all it indicated that Linden had been well aware for almost a week that the key piece of evidence that supported the suicide theory -- the locked bedroom door -- was not proof that a suicide had taken place, because the open windows in the bedroom clearly offered an alternate means of escape for a murderer. And there is little doubt that he was also aware that the bathroom door that opened out into the corridor offered yet another means by which a killer could escape.

But more important than that, here was the first indication that Linden and Wormley had been suppressing evidence of a possible murder in order to steer the investigation toward suicide.

It must be noted, however, that the fact that the windows were open is not proof that a murderer had climbed out one of them. The importance of the windows are that they cast doubt on the locked door as conclusive proof of suicide, and they suggest that Linden was part of a conspiracy to cover up what really happened in Room 57.

The McDermott interview also casts a shadow over Linden's reputation and raises questions about the way he handled the case. McDermott's belief that Linden was saying the opposite of what he believed in order to turn public attention away from the possibility of murder is certainly compatible with the way Linden had behaved throughout the investigation.

McDermott's criticism of Linden was a departure from the cozy relationship he had with Linden during the Gowen war on the Molly Maguires.

Back then McDermott had teamed up with Archbishop Wood of Philadelphia and Robert Linden to insure that the Mollys went to the gallows, but on the eve of the executions McDermott claimed that at least two of the Mollys, and maybe more, were innocent.

Yet, here in this article, he refused to answer a question about the guilt or innocence of the Mollys, even though he went public on the issue in 1877, which would indicate that the executions, and his part in them, were a serious problem for him by 1889.

The final item of interest in the McDermott interview was his statement -- "No such organization as the Molly Maguires ever existed. The only order was the Ancient Order of Hibernians."

This statement is of vast importance to those who study the Molly Maguire era.

Here is the ultimate insider, who was in the forefront of the Gowen/Pinkerton battle against the Molly Maguires, saying the Mollys never existed as an organization.

The issue of whether there was an organization named the Molly Maguires was a key issue in the defense of the Irish mine workers who were tried and executed in 1877 by the Linden/ Gowen combination. The defense claimed no such organization existed and the name was tagged on the defendants just to prejudice juries against them. It modern times it would be like tagging every Italian-American defendant a "Mafioso." All the defendants acknowledged membership in the Ancient Order of Hibernians (AOH), but no defendant admitted to being a Molly Maguire.

But McDermott's statement in *The Herald* was ignored by the rest of the newspapers, including those in the coal regions, which was surprising given the importance of the statement.

FRANCIS INNES GOWEN

Francis Innes Gowen was the quiet man of the entire Franklin Gowen murder/suicide investigation. There is little doubt that he was the power behind the investigation because he hired Linden and made no public attempt to rein in Linden when Linden's conclusions about Gowen's death were in conflict of the views of Mrs. Gowen, Esther Gowen, Franklin's daughter, and the views of Henry Gowen, Franklin's brother.

Instead he moved quietly in the background, taking over complete control of Franklin Gowen's law practice and immediately going into probate court to administer Franklin Gowen's estate.

While Mrs. Gowen and her daughter fought a very public battle to squash the suicide verdict, he gave no interviews to the press and made no attempt to openly manipulate the public perception of his uncle's death.

Who was this Francis Innes Gowen and what part did he play in the Gowen family saga?

Francis Innes Gowen was the son of James Emmett Gowen, deceased brother of Franklin B. Gowen. Francis Innes Gowen had been a junior partner in his father's law firm until the father died in 1885 at the age of 56. Then he joined Franklin Gowen's firm as a junior partner.[100]

Prior to Franklin Gowen's death, Francis Gowen lived in the long shadow cast by his uncle's reputation. Although he was 34-years-old when his uncle died and a brilliant lawyer in his own right, he had great difficulty in establishing a reputation for himself and was always known professionally and personally as the nephew of the great Franklin Gowen.

[100] Gowen Research Foundation, Lubbock, TX.

There is little doubt that had Franklin Gowen not been murdered that Francis Innes Gowen's career would have continued to be dominated by his uncle's image.

It must have been very difficult for Francis Innes Gowen to live in the shadow of his uncle. Franklin Gowen insisted that he run the office as he saw fit and there was no possibility of sharing authority with his junior partner. Franklin Gowen also was addicted to personal publicity and much of his time was spent away from the office on high profile cases while the younger Gowen labored in the Philadelphia office with less glamorous chores.

Shortly after Franklin Gowen died Francis Innes Gowen emerged from his uncle's shadow and established his own law office, with James Hood and Charles E. Ingersol as junior partners.[101]

But several years later he followed in Franklin Gowen's footsteps into the coal and railroad business, and it is amazing how similar his career was to that of his famous uncle.

In 1893, the Choctaw Coal & Railroad Company was reorganized as the Choctaw, Oklahoma and Gulf Railroad, and Francis Innes Gowen was named president. During a period of intense coal mining in Oklahoma he established a town in the eastern section of the state and named it Gowen after his family.[102]

Unlike his uncle, Francis Gowen appeared to be a careful and competent manager who kept his eye on the bottom line and engaged in none of the questionable business activities that led to his uncle's downfall.

[101] Gowen research Foundation.

[102] Ibid.

Although he became very prominent in his own right, Francis Gowen did not seek out publicity for its own sake, with the result his name was rarely in the papers.

Perhaps the biggest difference between the two men was that Francis Gowen lacked the brutal streak that Franklin exhibited during his war with the Molly Maguires.

Francis Gowen seemed to be in favor of compromise instead of confrontation, and he enjoyed a long and productive career. He went on to make a major mark in the business life of Philadelphia later in life. He was General Solicitor for the Philadelphia & Reading until 1912; he was a director of the Girard Trust Company and Midland Valley Railroad Company; he was manager of the Philadelphia Saving Fund Society.[103]

Gowen married Alice Robinson in 1884 and their descendants married into the Duponts and Goodyears and continued on the family tradition of being prominent in Philadelphia social circles.

However, in spite of his success later in life, Francis Gowen was a late bloomer, who was still playing second fiddle to his uncle at the age of 34. Compare this to the career of his grandfather James Emmet Gowen, who was out on his own in County Tyrone, Ireland, while still in his teens, and was in Philadelphia building a fortune while still in his twenties. [104]

Or compare it to the career of Franklin Gowen who had been sent out on his own at the age of thirteen, and had his own company at the age of 20. At the age of 24, Franklin Gowen had his own law firm, and was on his way to the presidency of the Reading while in his early thirties.[105]

[103] Gowen Research Foundation.

[104] Schlegel, *The Ruler of the Reading.*

[105] Ibid

None of this drive to succeed was evident in Francis Gowen until December 1889, when Franklin Gowen abruptly departed this life and Francis Gowen had to take responsibility for his own career.

Given Francis Gowen's talents and intelligence, it is difficult to understand why he had such a low profile in the days after his uncle was found dead.

It seems obvious that he should have been aware that the way Linden was handling the case would bring results which the rest of the Gowen family would not agree with.

However, it is possible that Francis Gowen's low profile was a deliberate strategy and that he was really in charge of the way that Gowen's death was being presented and that Linden was only following orders when he conducted the investigation in the way he did.

Captain Robert Linden was described by one reporter during the investigation as being "very deep" and that it was almost impossible to deduce what was on his mind.

The same might be said about Francis Innes Gowen.

*

PART TWO

DIFFERENT POINTS OF VIEW

The burial of Franklin Gowen put an end to much of the public debate on whether Gowen had committed suicide. Even though some members of the Gowen family continued to insist that "the facts were against an assumption of suicide," Robert Linden had prevailed in selling to the American public the theory that "the facts" pointed clearly to suicide.

In spite of their differences of opinion, it would seem that both Linden and the Gowen family were looking at the same body of information on Gowen's death that had been published in the newspapers, but were interpreting these "facts" in different ways. However, it is possible that both parties to the disagreement may have been in possession of information not published in the papers, and this information could have shed a new interpretation on Gowen's death. But no statements were issued by either party that indicated that there was evidence in existence that was not being made available to the public.

In order to make some sense of why Linden and some of the Gowens were in complete disagreement about the evidence, it would be useful to present Linden's argument on why he concluded that Gowen had committed suicide, and then follow up with Mrs. Gowen's view of the case.

First, Linden's point of view. He argued that Gowen's body was found in a room locked from the inside and he said he was aware of no credible evidence that a murderer could have exited the room from any other exit.

Linden said he was convinced a 38 mm Smith & Wesson was bought by Gowen from Walford, the gun dealer, and that this was the same gun that was used to take Gowen's life.

Linden said he could give no *reason* why Gowen took his life, but it was his opinion that the lawyer had suffered a bout of temporary insanity and during this time decided to do away with himself.

Linden went on to say that at the request of the Gowen family he had investigated the possibility that Gowen had been killed by the Molly Maguires but in spite of a thorough investigation no evidence that the Mollys were involved was unearthed. So, he could only come to the conclusion that Gowen had killed himself. He did not however, give any details of his Molly investigation or give any names of those under investigation.

The argument presented by Linden was straight forward and it made sense to most of those who were aware of it. As a rule most people will accept an argument that sounds reasonable and only a few will focus on the weakness of the argument.

As for the Gowen family point of view, the Gowens had stated frequently all the reasons why they believed Franklin Gowen would never have committed suicide, but members of the family had not been specific about describing the details that they believed clearly pointed to murder.

The Gowen argument is not very convincing since the absence of a reason for suicide is not proof of murder. Other than their personal opinion and the opinion of their closest friends the family offered no conclusive proof that Gowen did not in fact commit suicide. The family seemed to think that the evidence pointing to murder should have been obvious to everyone who was in possession of all the details of the case, and they acted as if they were bewildered why anyone would come to the conclusion that Franklin Gowen had taken his own life.

Thus, in the end, the conclusions arrived at by both sides to the dispute seemed to be based on personal opinion and not on any indisputable evidence offered that supported either theory.

Fortunately for those who have an interest in the Gowen case, the newspapers of the time presented most of the details of the case, thus making possible an independent evaluation of the evidence that is not based on the views of a reporter or the emotional reaction of members of the Gowen family.

In addition to the details, the sketch made of the room by *The Star* reporter is invaluable because it presents information that was obviously not focused on by anyone involved in evaluating the case, and these details reveal evidence that is not subject to debate.[106]

The sketch portrays various items in the room: doors, windows, a bureau, the bed, a table, a lamp, a fireplace with a mirror above it, a wardrobe, and blinds and curtains on the windows. The sketch also outlines where the body was lying; where the pistol was lying; and the location of the blood spots on the floor.

In addition to the above, the sketch outlines the bathroom connected to the bedroom, which contained a bath, a window overlooking an alleyway and a door leading out to the corridor. Directly across the corridor was a door leading to a fire escape.

The Star reporter had been in the room twice: once shortly after the body had been discovered, before either the coroner or Linden had seen the room; the second time just after the coroner had left, about 5 PM.

This early edition noted that the carpet had already been removed from the floor and that workmen were busy removing the wallpaper. The sketch was used by the reporter two days later to reinforce his argument that Gowen had committed suicide and that a murderer could not have escaped from the scene, but inadvertently the sketch clearly shows that the suicide theory was not as watertight as the reporter thought it was.[107]

[106] *The Star,* December 18, 1889.
[107] Ibid.

In the following segments of this chapter an analyses of all the evidence presented by the *Star* reporter will be provided, and this analysis will reveal that some of the most important evidence was not focused on at all.

An Analysis of the Evidence

The following items of evidence are divided into two groups. The first group consists of evidence already examined in some detail in earlier chapters, but will be examined in more detail now. This evidence include all exits from the room; the gun; the gaslight; and the wound, which was the subject of so much debate.

The second group consists of items that were mentioned only briefly in earlier chapters. These include an analysis of the blood stains; the position of the body; the condition of the bed; and the failure to hear a gunshot by any witness.

THE EXITS

It has already been pointed out that a murderer could easily have exited through the bathroom door and left the hotel via the fire escape, so this does not make the locked bedroom door conclusive proof that Gowen committed suicide. However, the availability of the bathroom exit is not proof that this exit was in fact used by a murderer.

It has also been pointed out that there is no evidence that it was Gowen who locked the door in the first place -- it could just as easily have been an assassin who locked the door in order to delay anyone finding Gowen's body. The hotel maid, the last person to see Gowen alive, other than the murderer, if there was a murderer, stated that when she spoke to Gowen at 3:30 PM, the door was not locked.[108]

[108] *The Star*, December 14, 1889.

A further issue involving the locked door raises the question: why would a man who was determined to do away with himself lock the door in order to delay the discovery of his body? What would have been the motive? Some might argue that he just wanted privacy to kill himself, but that privacy was provided by the closed door, because no staff member or friend ever walked into a bedroom without knocking first and getting permission to enter. And once the deed was done why would Gowen want to make it difficult to find his body?

The two windows in the bedroom were dismissed as possible escapes from the room on the grounds that they were closed and there were no scuff marks on the ledge of either window. The reporter wrote that there appeared to be no item in the room to anchor a rope that would have been used to facilitate an escape. He ignored the massive bureau and the heavy bed. But Linden admitted to a reporter from the *New York Herald* that the windows were not closed and therefore could have been used as a means of escape.[109]

The bathroom window, which was open three inches, was also ignored even though the bath would have made a perfect anchor for any rope used in an escape, and there was no mention made about whether there were scuff marks on the window ledge.

However, there would have been no reason for an intruder to go out that window, even if he could have done so, when he could have easily gone out the bathroom door.

Nevertheless, the dismissal of the windows as a means of escape, when in fact they could have been used for this purpose, is another indication that all of the evidence was not reviewed carefully before a decision was made to call Gowen's death a suicide.

[109] *New York Herald,* December 23, 1889.

THE GUN

The 38-mm Smith & Wesson found by Gowen's side was, in addition to the locked bedroom door, part of the foundation on which the suicide theory rested. The role played by the gun in this theory is as follows: The gun with the blood-stained handle was found by Gowen's side in the bedroom; it was confirmed by Linden that this gun was purchased from D. N. Walford,[or Mr. Smoot-- depending on which version you accept] who was convinced that Gowen may have been the man who bought this gun; therefore, it was assumed Gowen bought the gun in order to commit suicide.

These seemed reasonable assumptions to make, especially when linked to the fact that Gowen was found in a room with a locked door, and if no details are provided that might cast doubt on this evidence there was no reason why the average citizen would think of disputing these assumptions.

But again it is one thing to make reasonable assumptions, and another matter entirely to assume this evidence constitutes conclusive proof, especially when there are other ways to interpret this evidence that could lead to contradictory assumptions.

Finally, there were a number of unresolved issues about the gun that would have to have been solved before the gun could be used as conclusive proof that Gowen used it to commit suicide. Among these are the following.

* Walford gave conflicting evidence about the day and time that the gun was purchased. First, he identified the man who purchased the gun as Judge Montgomery, and then changed this identification to Franklin Gowen.

* Smoot told the police early Saturday evening that he had sold the gun and that he was alone in the store when the purchase was made. He could not positively identify Gowen as the man who bought the gun.

*   There were no witnesses who could confirm that Gowen left the hotel on either Thursday or Friday evening to purchase the gun, even though Gowen would have had to pass through the lobby which always had a doorman and clerk on duty.

*   Even if Gowen did purchase the gun there is no proof that he fired the gun, or proof that he intended to use it to commit suicide. Given the number of Molly Maguire threats he claimed to have received prior to his death he could have purchased the gun to defend himself.

*   There were no ballistic tests, which would prove the gun had been fired, and no retrieval of the bullet or bullets to prove they were fired from this particular gun. Furthermore there was no attempt to retrieve the bullet that caused the fatal wound even though it must have been lodged in the floor or in one of the walls.

*   The most critical issue of all, however, was the presence of blood on the handle -- so much blood in fact that it soaked the surface of the handle and even found its way underneath the pearl handle, as became evident when Walford unscrewed the handle in the store. What was the significance of this blood? The significance is as follows:

If Gowen had placed the muzzle of the gun against his head and pulled the trigger the bullet would immediately have driven the broken skin, tissue, bone and blood ahead of it into the wound, while at the same time rendering Gowen unconscious, which in turn would have caused the gun to fall out of his hand toward the floor.

Blood would then have emerged from both the entrance wound and the exit wound after the initial shock of the bullet entering the skull, but by this time the gun would have been on the floor near his waist, well away from any blood flow from the head.

So, where did the blood on the handle come from? There was no bloodstain on the floor near the gun, and in order to be soaked in blood the gun would have to have been sitting in a pool of blood.

There is a possible explanation for this, but it will be presented when the other issues involving the flow of blood from the wound are examined later.

THE GAS LIGHT

The unlit gas reading lamp on the desk in the bedroom had been used as proof that murder had been committed until Linden manipulated the time that the suicide was supposed to have taken place. After that the unlit lamp disappeared into the background, not to be mentioned again.

But the theory promoted by both Linden and Coroner Patterson -- that the lamp was not lit when Gowen died because Gowen shot himself in broad day light -- is questionable because of the fact that the blinds were drawn and the drapes were almost completely closed.

If the statements made by Wormley and Patrolman Cross are taken at face value-- that the drapes were almost closed and the blinds pulled down when Gowen's body was discovered on Saturday at noon -- then it can be assumed that very little daylight was being admitted into the room, and very little light would have been admitted into the room the previous afternoon when Gowen died.[110]

[110] *The Star*, December 14, 1889.

There may have been enough light for Gowen to direct the pistol to his head, but there certainly would not be enough light for him to work on the papers he was busy working on when his client, Mr. Rice, visited him at 1 PM, or when the maid visited him at 3:30 PM. He would have needed that light on in order to read.

So, if the light was off shortly before Gowen shot himself, who shut it off? Gowen himself? Why would he get up from his work... pick up his pistol ... lock the door ... and then shut off the light before walking over to the mirror over the fireplace in order to shoot himself?

This scenario just does not make sense, and if Gowen did shoot himself, the light must have been on at the time. So, back to square one. Linden initially said the unlit lamp pointed to a murder because Gowen could not have shut the light off after he shot himself. And yet the light was off.

A REVIEW OF THE EVIDENCE SO FAR

A review of the evidence up to this point indicates that the items that were presented by the coroner and by Linden as proof of suicide do not hold up under an in-depth analysis. The locked door is not proof of suicide because there was other exits available in the suite. The wound in the head could have been self inflicted, but it is highly unlikely.

There is no proof that Gowen bought the gun; no proof that he used it; no proof that this was the gun that inflicted the fatal wound. It is possible another gun fired the fatal shot and a person other than Gowen was involved in the shooting.

The unlit light was at first used as proof of murder, then was made a non-issue by the new Linden timelines, but the light arrived back as a possible indication of murder because of the drawn curtains and the blinds pulled down.

So, all the evidence presented so far does not prove anything if one is objective about the evidence. None of it proves Gowen committed suicide, but on the other hand none of it proves a murder was committed either, and without evidence that is not open to different interpretations one cannot, at this point, come up with an interpretation of Gowen's death that is not open to dispute.

There is one aspect of the evidence, however, that was ignored or misinterpreted, and this is the evidence that points to a conclusion that is not ambiguous, because it rules out suicide and clearly points toward murder. This is the evidence involving the blood stains in the room, which seemed to attract nobody's attention.

The Blood Stains

The blood on Franklin Gowen's clothes and the blood stains on the gun and in other parts of the room would have been a major issue if Gowen's death had occured in the United States today.

But the police, the coroner or Linden had nothing at all to say about this particular aspect of the crime scene, and yet this evidence is central to interpreting how Gowen met his death.

In some of the most celebrated murders publicized in modern times blood stains have often played a key part in solving the crime, and yet in the Gowen case there was blood all over the place but there was no effort made to determine what, if any, significance these blood stains might have had in solving the case.

There were blood stains in several areas of the room, as well as on different parts of Gowen's body, and each of these stains is significant in its own right.

The distribution of stains was as follows: massive soaking of Gowen's shirt, vest and underclothes; smaller stains on the floor beneath his head; a sprinkling of stains on the fireplace; a considerable amount of blood on the gun handle; a blob of blood at the foot of the bureau.

The blob of blood at the foot of the bureau, which was noticed by those who first entered the room, was a clear indication that it did not get there as a result of Gowen's suicide. This blood could not have been driven out of Gowen's head by the bullet and sent flying across the room because the bureau was to Gowen's right and the trajectory of the bullet was in the opposite direction.

The blood appears to have been carried over to the bureau area by someone stepping in Gowen's blood and carrying the blood across the room on his or her shoes. Since Gowen could hardly have stepped in his own blood after he shot himself, then this must have occurred when some other person stepped in his blood after he died, but before the body was "discovered" on Saturday afternoon.

[111] *The Star,* December 18, 1889.

Clearly, then, the death scene had been seriously violated by a person or persons unknown before Wormley and Patrolman Cross entered the room on Saturday at noon.

The blood splatters on the face of the fireplace and on the hearth are also incompatible with a scenario in which someone stands facing the fireplace and sends a bullet directly into his skull. The splattering that would occur as a result of this scenario would have sent blood and bone and tissue debris from the exit wound out on a trajectory that would be generally on a course parallel to the fireplace not directly onto it. It is possible, and indeed probable, that a degree of fanning out of the debris would occur after a short distance and this could send debris of to the right or left of a straight line, but given the location of the body, this could not occur until after the debris had cleared the fireplace.

The conclusion? Gowen would have to have been shot in another location, with the side of his head facing the fireplace in order for the trajectory of the blood spots to wind up on the front of the fireplace.

Next there is the blood on Gowen's clothing. There are several eyewitness descriptions of the fact that Gowen's coat, vest and underwear were soaked in blood. These descriptions also noted that the carpet beneath Gowen's head had bloodstains, but no stains were noted on the carpet beneath the blood-soaked body.[112]

What is wrong with this description provided by both reporters and police? Two problems are evident.

First, if the bloodstained head had stained the carpet, then one would imagine that some blood would have also filtered down from the blood-stained outer clothes and vest to the carpet beneath. But the carpet examined by a reporter shortly after it was removed from the floor reveals no such stain in the area of the carpet where the body had lain.

[112] *The Star,* December 18, 1889.

But there is a more important question -- how could the coat, vest and underclothes have become blood-soaked in the first place?

If one subscribes to the Linden's theory about the suicide, the blood-soaked clothing becomes a serious problem.

Again, according to the Linden theory, Gowen had got up from his desk, picked up his gun, locked the bedroom door, walked across the room toward the fireplace, stood in front of the mirror hanging above the fireplace, looked into the mirror and placed the gun to his head and pulled the trigger.

Gowen then fell to the floor and landed on his back, with the back of his head resting on the floor.

In this scenario, the blood would start pouring out of the head wound and the force of gravity would force the blood from the head wound to flow *down* to the carpet, where it should have created an enormous puddle of blood. But no enormous puddle of blood was evident on the carpet. Just two relatively small stains.

This, however, begs the question ...   where did the blood, which soaked Gowen's clothing, come from?   There was a slight upward incline from the head to the chest, and it would be impossible for the blood to flow *down* his cheek to the carpet, making only a small stain, while defying gravity to flow *upwards* across his face to soak the clothing on the body.

This is a key question to the riddle of Gowen's death, and one, which was not focused upon at all by any observer.

The amount of blood on the clothing also should have merited an examination of the body of Franklin Gowen to determine if, in fact, he had been struck on the chest by a bullet or bullets. This would have been incompatible with the suicide theory, but this was not focused on either.

Next there is a problem with the blood-soaked gun handle.

The presence of blood in copious amounts on the handle of the gun did not generate any comments either from the coroner, or from Linden, or from the police, except to point to the existence of the blood on the handle of the gun as proof that Gowen had committed suicide.

However, a competent medical examiner or an experienced detective would have many questions about this fact.

In order to show how this issue is important we must go back once again to the Wormley/Patterson/Linden account of how Franklin Gowen met his end.

According to the official theory, Gowen placed the gun close against his head and pulled the trigger. The gun had been so tightly placed against the head -- said the coroner -- that all the debris -- powder, etc -- was driven into the wound, leaving the entrance to the wound free of burns or powder marks.

Once the bullet entered the brain, Gowen would lose consciousness and begin to fall downwards, the gun falling away from his hand and dropping to the floor beside his body. His right hand fell beside the pistol.

Now, the question is this. Where did the blood come from that soaked the handle of the pistol? If the gun was held so tightly against the head that the bullet drove all debris ahead of it into the wound, how could the blood come out of the wound at the same time and soak the *handle* of the gun, which must have been six inches away from the muzzle of the pistol, while the pistol was spiraling toward the floor? And why was there no blood on the barrel of the gun?

Obviously the Linden/Patterson scenario just does not work -- it does not shed light on how the blood arrived in those various locations, so the distribution of the blood requires another ex- explanation.

Critical Issues

The blood on the clothing, the blood near the bureau, the blood on the fireplace, and the blood on the gun handle are critical items of evidence because they clearly demonstrate that blood could not have got on these locations if Gowen had committed suicide by standing in front of the mirror and shooting himself.

So, what are the implications of those items of evidence involving the blood?

The implications are as follows: if the blood on Gowen's clothing could not have flowed there while Gowen lay flat on his back on the floor, then Gowen must have been in another position entirely when the bullet entered his skull -- like, for instance, sitting on a chair at his desk.

If Gowen was in the chair when the fatal shot was fired, then the blood would have poured out of the head wound and down his face and neck and onto his jacket, shirt and underclothes. It would also have flowed directly to the floor, and if the pistol had been dropped on the floor beside the chair it could have soaked the handle. And if his head was turned slightly to his right when the bullet entered his head, a splatter of blood could have squirted over toward the fireplace.

This is the only way to explain the blood on the fireplace, on the gun, and on the clothing. And unlike the suicide theory involving the locked bedroom door, the unlit lamp, or the wound controversy this explanation is not open to more than one interpretation.

If Gowen had been sitting in the chair when the bullet entered his head killing him, and yet the body ended up on its back on the floor, it is obvious, then, that the body had to have been moved from the chair to the floor prior to it being first "discovered." And since Gowen could hardly have moved himself from the original position after being shot in the head, whoever moved the body was part of a conspiracy to conceal the true nature of Gowen's death.

The question is ... how could many of the doctors, detectives, and other experts who were aware of all the details on how Gowen's body was positioned in the bedroom have not been aware that there was something seriously wrong with the coroner's account of what happened in Room 57?

And why was there no serious challenge to the way Linden handled the case?

These remain the most puzzling aspects of the death of Franklin Gowen.

A SCENARIO WITHOUT CONTRADICTIONS

If the death scene scenario that was presented by Wormley, Linden and Coroner Patterson was so full of contradictions and impossibilities, was there a scenario that would resolve the issues that arose at the time of Gowen's death?

The following scenario comes close to solving them.

At 2:30 PM the maid at the Wormley Hotel knocked at the door of Room 57, about to enter the room and make the bed. The door was not locked. She had the door partially opened when Gowen, who was sitting at the desk near the door, told her to come back later because he was busy writing a report.

At 3:30 PM, she returned to the door and received the same reception from Gowen and she went off to clean other rooms.

Between 3:30 PM and 4:30 PM a person entered Gowen's room and during that person's presence in the room one or more pistol shots were fired at Gowen, one of which struck him above and behind the right ear, exiting through the left ear.

Fatally wounded, Gowen slumped in the chair, collapsing over the desk, knocking the desk lamp to the floor. Blood poured out of his head, down his cheeks and onto his jacket, his vest and his underwear, soaking them.

The killer locked the door from the inside to prevent being quickly discovered and then switched off the gas light to prevent a fire from breaking out.

What happened next depends a great deal on who the killer was and why he or she had killed Gowen.

At this point it would be productive to list the possible suspects in Gowen's murder and then eliminate those that can be eliminated by the evidence already at hand.

Among the possible suspects are a Molly Maguire; a bankrupt businessman; a close associate of Gowen's; or a disgruntled lover.

Suppose the killer was a Molly Maguire, what would the killer have done immediately after shooting Gowen? In all probability the killer would have left the room with all possible speed leaving the body where it was. A Molly would have no motivation for staging an elaborate suicide scenario because he would want the world to know Gowen had paid a heavy price for the Molly executions.

What are the chances this was a Molly murder? Practically nil, because if the Mollys had killed Gowen, nobody would have moved the body to try and make it look like a suicide, and anyway, if the Gowens and Linden were really convinced this was a Molly Maguire murder they would search the world to find the killer. So, the Mollys had nothing to do with Gowen's death, and Linden and Francis Innes Gowen knew this from the very beginning.

Next, there is the possibility than a bankrupt businessman visited Gowen and got into a confrontation with him over a lost fortune, either shooting him with Gowen's own gun, or shooting him with a gun he had brought with him.

If this had happened, he, too, would have fled the scene immediately after the killing, and he would have no reason either to stage a suicide scenario.

Was such a businessman a viable suspect? Hardly, because again Linden and the Gowen family would have gone after him and prosecuted him to the full extent of the law.

A close associate of Gowen's who had a deep grudge against the financier would also have a motive for the killing, but again who would cover up for such a person and why? If this suspect was a Gowen relative, there might be a temptation for Francis Innes Gowen to hire Linden to cover up the crime, but why would Wormley risk the gallows by being involved in such a conspiracy?

This leaves only one possible type of suspect: a disgruntled lover who killed Gowen either deliberately or accidentally, and if this lover was a "sex for sale" lover, there is a possibility that Francis Gowen, Linden and, indeed, Wormley would get together to hide the true nature of Gowen's death from the public, and even from the rest of the Gowen family, because this would be even more embarrassing to the family than a suicide.

Why would Wormley willingly get involved in the conspiracy? He did so because he faced ruin if the word got out that "ladies of the night" were murdering guests in the Wormley Hotel.

The above scenario is pure speculation, but it is the only scenario that makes it credible that Francis Gowen, Linden and Wormley entered into a conspiracy to conceal the nature of Gowen's death, and if this was not the scenario, then it must have been a different scenario that contained the same basic elements: Gowen met his death in bizarre circumstances that would bring disgrace to both the Gowens and the Wormleys -- a disgrace worse than a suicide -- and Linden was called in to muddy the waters.

Who Moved the body?

It is very unlikely that a killer who had not planned this killing, but instead killed during a disagreement with Gowen had the presence of mind to move the body from the chair to the floor before fleeing the room in order to make Gowen's death look like a suicide. Panic and an urge to get out of there in order not to get caught would have been the dominant state of mind. So, the body was left in the chair, the blood oozing out of it.

So what happened next? The following is a possible scenario.

When the maid returned to the room at 4:30 PM and 6 PM she found the door locked and no response to her knocks.

After she tried the door for the last time that day, it would have been her duty to tell either the head clerk or Wormley about the silence in Room 57 and her inability to make the bed before she went home for the night. It would have been her duty to do so because the Wormley Hotel was a first class hotel that prided itself on service, and other hotel staff would be designated to follow up later on to see what the problem was in Room 57.

After the maid reported that there was no response from Gowen's room on Friday evening, Wormley or the head clerk took the key for Gowen's bathroom door from the office and went up and entered the bedroom suite through the bathroom and found Gowen slumped over his desk, his clothes soaked in blood and his brains seeping out of his skull.

Either Wormley or the head clerk would have known the name of Gowen's last visitor, because all visitors had to go through the lobby, and if this visitor was a woman, and there had been a report earlier of a noisy quarrel in Gowen's room, then this woman would have been the prime suspect in Gowen's killing. And if the woman was of questionable morals, then Wormley would know he had a major problem on his hands.

Wormley's dilemma would have been how to handle this horrific situation, and it is unlikely that whatever action he took he would have made a decision on his own.

Wormley's strategy would be to place a call to Francis Innes Gowen in Philadelphia and brief him on the catastrophe that had taken place. The Wormley Hotel was one of the first hotels in Washington to install a telephone, a new invention at the time, and no doubt a top law firm like the Gowen firm would also have a phone. Wormley would have asked for advice on how to handle the matter, and Francis Gowen, when he recovered from the shock, may have said he would seek the advice of Robert Linden and get back to him.

The advice must have been to stage a suicide -- a very undesirable strategy, but given the circumstances apparently more desirable than the reality. Wormley agreed to rearrange the death scene to make it look like a suicide, but did it in a very amateurish way.

A decision to delay the "discovery" of the body would have been agreed upon at this time, so that Francis Gowen and Linden would have time to work up a strategy for dealing with the situation.

This strategy included throwing the Molly Maguires out front as suspects in order to divert attention from any other suspects, and to wrap up Linden's investigation with all possible speed, in the hope that the truth would not get out.

Next morning when the maid returned to report on the continuing silence in Room 57, Wormley took the head porter, Patrolman Cross and another porter with him and using a stepladder he peered into the bedroom and "discovered" the body.

It is interesting that Wormley made no attempt to bring the key to the bathroom door with him, because this would have eliminated the need to climb through the transom, using a stepladder.

Within the hour the body was hurried out of the room and on its way down to the police station, at which point Wormley pulled up the carpet and tore down the wallpaper.

Why were the carpet and wallpaper removed? This is a key issue that has continued to haunt the Gowen story.

If there was no ulterior motive for tearing down the wallpaper and ripping up the carpet, then Wormley's actions were unfortunate to say the least, because they contributed to a perception that he was destroying important evidence by disturbing the crime scene in this manner.

What sort of evidence could have been destroyed in this manner? One possibility is that there were huge blood stains on the carpet underneath the chair and table, and Wormley would have disposed of this section of carpet before he allowed *The Star* reporter into the room. The carpet could have become soaked during the time Gowen's body was slumped in the chair, and the carpet had to be pulled up in order to hide these stains.

Another possibility is that the killer fired more than one shot at Gowen and the missed shots ploughed into the carpet or the walls. In order to prevent the discovery of bullet holes in the floors or walls, it was decided by those involved to destroy the evidence, because nothing would have destroyed a suicide theory so effectively as evidence that more than one bullet had been fired. The idea that Gowen had fired several shots at his own head -- and missed -- would hardly be accepted by even the most gullible members of the public.

So, by disturbing the crime scene it was made difficult to determine what had happened, although if the scene had been thoroughly investigated by detectives who had no private agenda then the evidence of what really happened would have emerged.

The scenario outlined above provides explanations for all the discrepancies surrounding the death of Franklin Gowen, without, however, providing the name of the killer. The scenario also provides an explanation for the way Linden, Wormley and Francis Gowen behaved, and why they were in such a hurry to promote the suicide theory.

The scenario above is compatible with the evidence, and if that was not the scenario then it must have been a scenario that contained the same basic elements: Gowen's murder involved such bizarre circumstances that it posed ruin for the Wormley Hotel and a bigger disgrace than suicide for the Gowen Family.

The problem with a "woman involved" theory is that, apart from the logic of the theory, there is little supporting evidence available, because there was not a hint in any of the newspapers that Gowen liked to amuse himself with female company when he was away from home. Not that it was likely that there would be any hints in the newspapers about his romances, either, because during this period this was a subject that was off limits to newspapers. It was not until the Kennedy era that the subject of sex and martial infidelity was seen as a legitimate story for the press.

So, even though this scenario fitted together as neatly as a jigsaw puzzle, I would have been far more comfortable if I could dig up some evidence that would support this part of my murder theory.

I knew that, realistically, this research into the death of Franklin Gowen seemed to have gone about as far as it could go, and it would be a long shot indeed if further research would turn up anything else.

However, because of the involvement of members of my family in the Molly Maguire saga, I disliked leaving the story hanging up there in mid air without making at least some effort to flesh out the story a little more, even though I knew the chances of finding out who killed Franklin Gowen were slim.

Apart from trying to find out the identity of the killer, I was also curious to discover which Molly suspects Robert Linden had investigated out in the coal regions, since I had numerous relatives out there at that time and, theoretically, any of them could have been suspects because of the Alec Campbell connection.

So, I decided to pursue the research a little further to see what I could turn up.

PART THREE

THE SEARCH TURNS PERSONAL

When I began to investigate the death of Franklin Gowen my goal was to determine if his death was the result of suicide or murder. I had no other goals beyond that. But once I had proved to my own satisfaction that he definitely did not kill himself, I was overcome with curiosity about who killed him and was tempted to continue the investigation.

However, I knew that launching an investigation into Gowen's death was a far more difficult chore than determining whether his death was a result of murder or suicide. In the first part of my investigation it was simply a matter of analyzing the evidence that had been provided by the newspapers -- there was not that much research involved and no digging into a case that had been cold for more than a hundred years and had been the result of a deliberate cover up. But I decided to go ahead with the project anyway.

To begin this new phase of the project, I decided to make a list of the people who, when they were alive, might have information about the death of Gowen that had never been revealed to the public. I also made a list of the places where files might still exist that could possibly contain some clues.

Since all of those directly involved were long dead, my plan was to find descendants who might be in possession of information that was handed down over the last 113 years.

I thought that locating the places where the files might be in city, state or national archives would not be a problem, and the list of names whose descendants I would pursue was relatively short: Captain Robert Linden, Francis Innes Gowen, and James Thompson Wormley.

The Descendants.

I had selected Linden for obvious reasons: he was in charge of the investigation from the beginning to the hour Gowen was buried; he had complete access to the crime scene; and he had interacted with the Gowen family and many of Gowen's friends, so if anyone was in possession of all the facts involved in Gowen's death, then it would be Robert Linden.

My pursuit of Linden would be mounted on several fronts: I had already met his grandson, an affable gentleman, now aged 80, after I had published *A Molly Maguire Story*, so I decided I would definitely call him up and see what, if anything, he could, or would tell me on the Gowen case. I also intended to track down whatever Pinkerton files were in existence and see if Linden had written any reports that would be housed in the archives.

I did not expect to get much information out of Linden's grandson, who was also named Robert Linden. I had met him several times over the years and our relationship had been very cordial, in spite of the fact that his grandfather had played a major role in sending my grand uncle to the gallows.

My attitude towards Linden was -- if you are polite to me then I will be polite to you. He seemed to have adapted the same attitude.

Nevertheless, I knew that Linden was proud of his grandfather even if he did not shout it from the rooftops. Several years ago he proved it when a mock trial was staged on the Alec Campbell case in the Carbon County Courthouse, Pennsylvania.

When the proceedings began, he stood up and demanded attention from Judge John Lavelle, who was staging the mock trial, and told Lavelle that he was there to see that his grandfather got a fair shake. Lavelle was surprised to see him there, as were many of the other people present.

However, I also found out later an item about Linden's background that few in the courtroom knew about that day. In addition to being the grandson of Captain Robert Linden, I also found out that his mother was an O'Donnell from Tamaqua, Pennsylvania.

The O'Donnell name was one that was carried by many of the Molly Maguires and since Linden was raised a Catholic he had a "mixed" heritage.

Over the years I learned that Linden seemed to have some affection for his Irish Catholic roots, so I was not really sure where in the final analysis Linden's strongest loyalties lay.

A few years after the mock trial, when a new AOH division was founded in Jim Thorpe-- a division named after Alec Campbell -- Linden was among those who signed up, but I do not think he was very active in the division, and he may have shown up in the first place just to "keep an eye on things."

I knew Robert Linden was in a very difficult position. On the one hand he was the grandson of a famous Pinkerton detective, and on the other hand it is possible that his grandfather or great grandfather could have been members of the AOH out in Schuykill County in the 1870s, an organization that Captain Robert Linden had destroyed. So, there were bound to be conflicting loyalties there somewhere.

I had maintained contact with Robert Linden over the years, exchanging letters and sometimes phone calls, but he had resisted -- very politely --any attempt on my part that we get together and get involved in a lengthy discussion about the Molly Maguires.

I have a good idea why he had no interest in a get-together, because it would have been a lose/lose situation for him, although there is little doubt that we would have had plenty to talk about.

In spite of this, I decided that I would go on a fishing expedition by calling up Linden and asking him a few questions about what he knew about Franklin Gowen's death.

As always, the conversation was pleasant, but non-productive. He seemed very surprised that I was convinced that Gowen had not committed suicide, but he did not argue with me about it.

When I told him that his grandfather had been going along with the suicide verdict when the evidence suggested otherwise, he said he thought that any position taken by his grandfather would have been the position that his clients wanted him to take.

"He would never work against the best interests of his client," Linden said. His client in this case was Francis Innes Gowen, who had brought him on board.

I thought that he was probably correct when he said that Captain Robert Linden was only following orders when he covered up the murder, but he could offer me no clue on who might have killed Gowen.

Linden changed the subject shortly after that and I knew he did not want to talk further about the Gowen affair. I wondered what he really knew about Gowen's death, but I also knew I would never find out any details from him. Like his grandfather, he was very deep and knew how to keep a secret.

The Wormleys.

The search for the descendants of James Thompson Wormley took up a great deal of time and effort and in the end showed as little reward as my talk with Robert Linden. But it was a search that was necessary since James Thompson Wormley was a major player in the Gowen story. I began the search by attempting to locate the Wormley Hotel in Washington, but a search of the Internet indicated that there was no such hotel in existence.

Then I contacted every Wormley in the telephone directories in New Jersey, New York, Pennsylvania, Maryland, and Washington D.C.

After that I went on the Internet and contacted every Wormley I could find, but had no luck.

Finally, I went down to Washington and went to the address given in the 1889 newspapers and discovered that the hotel had been demolished and a modern office building erected in its place.

A walk around the neighborhood produced no leads: I could find no one who had ever heard of James Wormley or the Wormley Hotel.

I thought it a little ironic -- here was an establishment that had been a Washington landmark one hundred years ago, known to every resident of the city, and now the building and the name had vanished without a trace.

I decided that there was not going to be any easy way of locating a Wormley descendant, and that if I did manage to turn one up it would be the result of hard work... and a little bit of luck.

Next I tried a new line of investigation, using a different strategy. Since Wormley was a Black American and was famous in his time, I decided to go to the local library and locate a *Who's Who* of prominent Americans. I thought that such a publication might mention the Wormley Family. I was right.[113]

There was a considerable amount of information on members of the Wormley Family, including James Wormley, father of James Thompson Wormley, and this provided further leads on the history of the family.[114]

[113] *Who's Who in America*

[114] *Journal of Negro History, April 1935*
Journal of Negro History, Jan 1936
Evening Star{Washington] Oct 17, 18, 20, 25, 1884.
Washington Post, Oct. 18, 20. 1884

As I pursued this research, I was to discover that the Wormley family had not only distinguished themselves in the Nineteenth century, but their descendants had continued to forge successful careers in medicine, law, business and commerce in the Twentieth Century and was continuing this success story in the Twenty First Century. Among the distinguished members of the family are, to name two, Stanton Wormley Sr., and Donet Graves.

Stanton Wormley Sr., who had, prior to his death in 1993, been a professor of German and Russian Studies at Howard University and had also served as acting university president between 1965 and 1967. He was active in many civic organizations, including the National Conference of Christians and Jews and was the author of several books.

Donet Graves, of Cleveland Heights, Ohio, is a managing partner in the law firm of Graves & Horton. He is the chairman of the Magistrate Selection Committee of the U.S. District Court for the Northern District of Ohio. He is also on the board of Trustees for the United Black Fund and for the Committee for Public Art.

When I sent a written inquiry to Mrs. Stanton Wormley at her Washington home, I was contacted by a representative of the Wormley Family who was compiling a family tree of the Wormleys, one branch of which went back to England in the Twelfth century. He was very informed about all aspects of the family history but had never heard of Franklin Gowen, never mind have information about his death.

Donet Graves has studied the Wormley Family history in depth also and has amassed a huge collection of photographs of the Wormleys all the way back to the 1850s.

He knew all about the Wormley Hotel and James Thompson Wormley, but he had never come across the name Franklin Gowen and was very surprised to hear of the controversy that surrounded James Thompson Wormley in the days after Gowen's death.

Graves made a number of phone calls to see if any of his relatives had information about Gowen, but was unable to turn up anything. Gowen's name seemed completely unknown among the Wormley descendants.

*

Next, I made contact with two of the Gowen descendants, Francis Innes Gowen, grandson of Francis Innes Gowen who had been Franklin Gowen's nephew and law firm partner, and William Gowen, grand nephew of Franklin Gowen. Both were thoroughly familiar with the history of the Gowen family, but neither one could shed any light on Gowen's death, except to say that no reason had been handed down in the Gowen family folklore for Franklin's suicide. Both were surprised to hear that I believed he was murdered, but neither had any opinion about who the murderer might be.

The results of my interviews with the descendants of Linden, Wormley and Gowen were disappointing, although I did not really expect them to provide me with any information they had on his death if a scandal had been involved which cast an ancestor's image in an unflattering light.

The Archives.

Having struck out in my interviews with the descendants of the principal characters in the Franklin Gowen mystery, I decided that my next move would be to search a number of archives that might have some documentation on Gowen's death.

These archives included the police archives for the District of Columbia, the coroner's files for the same area; the Pinkerton archives; the Reading Railroad files; the National Archives; the Library of Congress archives; and the Rockefeller archives. I had targeted the Rockefeller archives because Gowen at the time of his death was involved in litigation with John D. Rockefeller.

I began my search of the archives by giving a priority to those archives that seemed the most likely to contain the type of information that I was seeking.

One of these archives was the archives of the Washington D.C. Police Department, which I thought might contain some files on the Gowen case.

During my initial investigation into Gowen's death, I discovered that there had been resistance by some members of the police to the idea that Gowen had committed suicide, and if these police officers believed that Gowen had been murdered, I wondered if they had written memos about who they suspected had killed him.

This seemed like an idea worth researching, so I embarked on a new phase of the project.

Being at this point relatively experienced at research, I did not think for one moment that I could call up the Washington Police... locate the archives ... and then, without any difficulty, find files that would give me answers to any questions I might have on Gowen's death. In real life, things never work out that way.

But I was not prepared for the frustration either of trying to locate the Washington police archives, which, after twenty calls, all I could determine was that no one in the city government seemed to know anything about them or where they were.

Eventually, however, I was told that all the files from the 1890s had been sent to the National Archives, and that I should switch my search to that facility.

The National Archives is an organization much better organized than the City of Washington, and in no time at all I was informed that while the facility did have police files for Washington, the files for December 1889 and January of 1890 were missing. I then asked if there were any files for the Coroner's office for 1889, but was told that they, too, were missing. I was told that a situation like this was typical: every year the National Archives receives mountains of documents that had been lying in city or state basements in no particular order and it was inevitable that some of them would go astray.

The thought crossed my mind that some researcher had got to these files while they were still in the custody of the Washington police and neglected to return them.

Either that or the files had been deliberately removed so that no one could find out what they contained.

So, I had come up with a total blank on a line of investigation that I thought might provide me with some valuable items of information.

My next focus of research was the Pinkerton archives, which I believed at this point were housed out in California.

I decided I had nothing to lose by calling up the archives and chatting to the person in charge.

My primary interest in getting access to the files was to determine what files, if any, were there that would shed some light on Linden's investigation of the Molly Maguires after Gowen had been found dead. I hoped to get Linden's reports on his investigation, and I also hoped to dig up the reports of the twelve Pinkerton agents in the field who were assigned to investigate various Molly Maguire suspects.

I had little problem getting through to the archivist, but I learned that the archives were no longer in California -- that they had been donated to the Library of Congress the previous year and were now being made available to the public to all those who wanted to go to Washington to review them.

When I told the archivist the nature of my research she told me that she did not think I would have much luck, because the Pinkertons had a policy of returning all files generated by any case to the client once the case was closed.

"Whatever files that would have been generated would have been given to the Gowen family," she said.

We talked about the Molly Maguires for some time and during this conversation she said she was amazed that the Mollys had never come after James McParland.

"You would think that they would have got revenge one way or the other."

She went on to say that according to material in the archives which she had read, McParland did not get much respect within the Pinkerton organization, because he was drunk most of the time and he was very difficult to get along with.

"They would have got rid of him if they could but he had this fantastic reputation because of the publicity he received in the Molly Maguire era, and they thought that if they dumped him that it would generate a great deal of bad publicity for the agency."

But McParland was generating bad publicity for the Pinkertons over the years anyway: first because he had retained the cowboy hitman Tom Horn to assassinate scores of cattle rustlers on behalf of the cattle barons, and later in the way he handled the Big Bill Haywood affair.[115]

[115]   J. Anthony Lukas. *Big Trouble*

Horn had a contract with the Pinkertons to kill any rustlers whose names were supplied by the cattle barons. Horn got $700 for each kill and McParland's agency got an additional $700 in commissions.[116]

Horn was doing very well until he killed a fourteen-year-old boy by mistake and went to the gallows for his crime.

The Pinkertons, led by McParland were also involved in a campaign to railroad Pettibone, Moyers and Haywood, the leaders of the Western Federation of Miners to the gallows, but the plot failed because the union hired famed American attorney Clarence Darrow to defend the union leaders and he won an acquittal. There was widespread condemnation of the Pinkertons at the time over the way they handled this case. [117]

After the acquittal, a McParland aide suggested that Moyers, Pettibone, and Haywood be assassinated, but after thinking about the idea for a while McParland vetoed the idea on the grounds that it would create bad publicity for the Pinkertons.

This gives some idea of the mentality of the Pinkertons over taking the lives of those that they considered enemies.

Anyway, after the Heywood affair, the Pinkerton management tried to ease McParland into retirement on the grounds that he had poor health. He did indeed have poor health caused by a lifetime of addiction to alcohol, but the Pinkerton management was only using his health as an excuse for getting rid of him.[118]

[116] Lukas, *Big Trouble.*

[117] Ibid.

[118] The letters and memos written by the Principals in the Pinkerton Agency pertaining to James McParland, which are part of the Pinkerton Papers in the Library of Congress collection, are laced with critical comments about the way McParland ran the Denver agency. In the last ten years of his career he did not receive a raise and clearly the owners of the agency wanted to get rid of him. But he would not leave.

But on the issue of the files generated by each case, I thought it a little strange that the Pinkertons would not keep a copy of the files on each case in their archives, and instead returned all the paperwork to the client. Somehow this seemed unreasonable to say the least. After all there had to have been a lot of mundane paperwork generated by each case, such as internal memos, book-keeping memos relating to fees, and private memos between Pinkerton agents and Pinkerton managers -- paperwork that would never normally be sent to a client.

So if this sort of paperwork was never normally sent to the client during the course of the case, why would it all be shipped off once the case was closed? This did not make sense.

But an expose entitled *Two Evilisms, Anarchism and Pinkertonism,* written by ex-Pinkerton detective Charles Seringo, who had worked under McParland, sheds light on the reason for missing files.

According to Siringo, it was a common practice to double bill clients for services -- billing for the time spent by two agents on a job when only one worked on the project.

There were other questionable practices such as framing criminals and giving evidence that was erroneous, so that it would be impractical, or even dangerous to keep these files around. It is possible therefore that all files were destroyed once a case was ended and were not, as the Pinkertons claimed, handed over to the clients.

Of course, another problem emerged from the continuous reports sent to the client as the case was in progress. If the internal reports were very different from the reports sent periodically to the client because McParland and his fellow managers were jazzing up the client reports to make the agency look good, then there would be a very good reason why all paperwork would have been shredded.

In spite of the fact that the manager of the Pinkerton archives warned me that I would find nothing of use in the Pinkerton papers in the Library of Congress, I made up my mind that at some point I would take a trip to Washington D.C. and take a look at the papers myself.

In Pursuit of Pinkerton Agents.

Meanwhile, I decided to focus on the activities of Linden's agents who went out into the coal fields in the period of 12/14/1889 to 12/18/1889. Linden had said that he had sent twelve of his best agents to canvass the area intensely in order to determine if any of the Mollys recently released from jail might have been involved in Gowen's murder.

I had already come to the conclusion that this Molly Maguire investigation was nothing more than a distraction to divert attention from the true nature of Gowen's death, but I still was curious to find out what type of investigation had been conducted.

My strategy for my investigation was to identify those libraries and historical societies in the coal regions that had on microfiche the local newspapers from 1889.

Once I had identified these sources I would visit each of them in turn and comb the newspapers for accounts of how the Pinkertons had conducted their investigation.

I felt reasonably certain that these papers would carry an abundance of accounts of the Pinkerton bloodhounds on the trail of the Mollys, because there was no reason why the editors of these newspapers should not have been beside themselves with excitement at the prospect of major Molly Maguire stories breaking in their area.

After all, the trial and execution of the Mollys in the 1870s had been front-page news for years and there was no reason to assume that in the decade that had passed since then that interest in the Mollys would have waned.

But on my first stop in the public library in Jim Thorpe[Mauch Chunk] I was to discover that the newspapers that had carried front page stories about the arrest, trial and execution of the Mollys in the years between 1875 and 1878, and about Gowen's relentless pursuit of them, just carried brief accounts of Gowen's death, which they classified as a suicide, and there was only a brief mention of the accusations being made in the Washington and Philadelphia newspapers that Gowen had been done in by the Molly Maguires. Nor was there any mention of Pinkerton agents out to the coal region area to question area residents-- residents who might very well have been readers of these newspapers.

The whole tone of the stories suggested that Gowen's death was of no interest to the citizens of Carbon County, a point of view that seemed removed from reality.

I knew that according to the folklore of the area handed down for generations later, when word reached Carbon County and other counties in the coal regions that Gowen had committed suicide, there was a grim satisfaction expressed among the Irish living in the area that the boss of the Reading had met a violent end. There certainly was no indication that the hatred of Gowen had lessened in intensity in the ten years since the executions, or that the Irish residents were in any mood to forgive him. Indeed it was rumored that a celebration of sorts had taken place that he was no longer in the land of the living.

It would seem likely therefore that the newspaper editors in Carbon County were well aware of the animosity among their Irish readers toward Gowen, and aware that they would be deeply interested in all details about how he met his death.

The German and Welsh communities should have been equally interested in the story and curious about who in their community might be questioned about Gowen's death.

But as far as the *Mauch Chunk Gazette* was concerned the Gowen death might have occurred in some remote area and both the victim and those suspected in his murder were strangers to the citizens of Carbon County for all the interest the paper displayed in the story.

An investigation of the papers in the Public Library in Pottsville did produce more extensive coverage, as did an investigation of the newspapers housed in the Luzerne County Historical Society in Wilkes-Barre. The coverage varied in the amount of space devoted to the story, but there was nothing written about a team of Pinkertons patrolling the coal regions or little credibility given to the rumors that a Molly had taken revenge on Gowen.

It is hard to understand the reason for this. Surely these detectives would have created some waves as they knocked on the doors of Molly relatives, or made contact with local law enforcement jurisdictions. Surely at some point a story should have been generated, even if it were only a couple of paragraphs in a weekly newspaper.

But I could find nothing at all printed during the two weeks after his death.

What was one to make of this?

I thought that there were three possible reasons for the lack of coverage, all of which could have resulted in a blackout.

First, it was possible that the Pinkertons had been so discrete that they had moved in and out of the coal regions without bringing themselves to the attention of anyone except the families they had interviewed.

Then, there might have been an understanding worked out between the editors of the region and Linden to play down the death of Gowen -- for reasons known only to themselves.

Finally, there was the possibility that Linden had not sent any detectives out to the coal regions at all.

If this were the case what would have been Linden's reason for not initiating the very investigation that the Gowen family had supposedly hired him to conduct, even if it was a sham investigation designed to divert suspicion from the real cause of Gowen's death?

I was not sure which of these options was the correct one, but I had a growing suspicion that the Pinkerton posse had not existed and was just a smokescreen created by Linden.

But I was unwilling to turn away from this particular issue until I tried another approach in order to see if I could gain some more insights into the way Linden had conducted the investigation.

Molly Descendants.

The new approach was to interview the descendants of the executed Mollys. During my years of research for *A Molly Maguire Story* I had contacted many of the descendants of the Mollys, and in the years since the book was published I had acquired many more names of people who possessed a vast amount of information about all aspects of the Molly story.

I believed that in all those names as well as the names of Alec Campbell's descendants I had a great resource that should be able to provide some information on the subject.

I began my new approach by calling up members of the various branches of the Campbell family who were the descendants of Rose, Annie and Alec Campbell. Rose and Annie were the sisters of Alec Campbell and many of their descendants had remained in the coal regions after the executions of the 1877. I followed this with calls to the descendants of other Mollys.

Life had been tough for the Campbells after the execution of Alec Campbell -- the reputation of being related to a killer was one they could not get rid of easily, even with the passing of generations. Even when members of the extended family went into the church as priests or nuns, the Alec Campbell story continued to haunt them and had a major effect on the way they were perceived, especially in the Welsh and German communities.

As time passed, the descendants defended themselves by keeping very quiet about Alec Campbell, and this was made easier by the fact that Sarah and Annie lost the Campbell name when they married, and Alec Campbell's daughter, Rose, was no longer a Campbell after she married.

The Alec Campbell story also faded away for another reason: parents in each succeeding generation shielded their children from the unsavory reputation of their ancestor by passing on very little about the Alec Campbell story

This scarcity of family folklore made it very difficult for me when I was researching *A Molly Maguire Story.* So I did not know how I would fare when I contacted them about the Pinkerton detectives. But I thought I had nothing to lose by making phone calls to see what I would turn up.

But after several weeks of playing telephone tag with relatives, I came up empty-handed, without even a hint from any branch of the family that the Pinkertons had been on the warpath back in 1889 and had talked to any of my relatives about the Franklin Gowen case.

It occurred to me that such a visit by the Pinkertons might not have been passed down in family folklore. It was bad enough to live with the accusation that Alec Campbell had been an accessory to the murder of Jack Jones and Morgan Powell without telling the children that members of the family were also suspects in the murder of Franklin Gowen.

Nevertheless, I found it hard to believe that not the slightest hint had seeped down among the Campbell descendants, or among the descendants of the other Mollys, about the Gowen killing, and this reinforced a growing conviction that Robert Linden may not have sent out any detectives to the coal regions at all, in spite of the fact that he had repeatedly told the national press that the Pinkerton agents were busy out in Pennsylvania. And Francis Innes Gowen must have known that the Pinkerton agents were not on the prowl out in the coal regions.

So, what was the truth about the alleged Molly investigation?

The scenario may have been as follows: Francis Gowen had called Linden on Friday evening and told him that he had received a call from Washington that informed him that Franklin Gowen had been killed under bizarre circumstances, and he enlisted Linden's assistance in handling the problem.

If the problem had been such that it could prove a major disgrace to the extended Gowen family, Linden's chore would have been to control the damage in the most effective way.

Supposing Gowen's death involved a woman, and the shooting had occurred accidentally when the woman was toying with Gowen's newly acquired pistol, or deliberately for reasons unknown, then the problem for Linden would be to present this death to the public in a way that would minimize the disgrace to the Gowen family.

The choices facing Linden and Francis Gowen were lose/lose choices. If the death were to be characterized as a murder there would be tremendous pressure to find the killer; if the death were to be characterized as a suicide, it would reflect badly on the Gowen family, but this would be nothing compared to the disgrace if it came out that a woman were involved. So, the suicide choice was the lesser of two evils.

Linden may have decided to entertain the Molly Maguire murder theory anyway simply because he knew others would come to that conclusion since Franklin Gowen was always telling his friends that he was receiving threats from the Molly Maguires. Gowen had in fact liked the image of a brave man been stalked by murderous thugs.

So, Linden decided to announce that he suspected the Molly Maguires and was launching an investigation and had sent twelve agents out into the coal regions to do an extensive investigation of selected Molly suspects, but this announcement was just a red herring and he had never any intention of sending agents out to the coal regions at all.

MY INVESTIGATION CONTINUES

My next line of investigation was to contact the Library of Congress and make inquires about the Pinkerton files that had been handed over to the Library in the summer of 2000.

The person I initially contacted was very helpful, promising me that all the files would be made available if I came down to Washington and browsed through them, but he warned me that the files consisted mainly of press cuttings and internal memos and that very little of substance on any particular case would be found in these files.

My main hope was that I would find some detailed information on the Gowen case in those files, in spite of the fact that I had been told by the Pinkerton archivist that all files involved in each Pinkerton case would have been returned to the client, which in this case was Francis Gowen.

So, it was with some anticipation that I made the 200-mile trip to Washington and ran a gauntlet of security clearances at the Library of Congress in order to gain access to the Pinkerton files, which were housed in scores of cardboard boxes and on microfiche tapes. This initial trip was the first of five trips in all that I made to Washington to review the Pinkerton archives.

The Library of Congress is managed by professionals who are very much into providing all the help they can to anyone who comes to them with a project. When the Pinkerton Files were donated to the facility, more than a year was spent organizing the files into a system that made it relatively easy for any researcher to retrieve information. And a guide to the files was created that provides an overview of the contents of the files, thus allowing the researcher to hone in on any particular subject.

My first review of the files focused on the name Franklin Gowen, but I soon discovered that Gowen's suicide/murder was not mentioned at all, even though there was material on hundreds of other famous cases.

There was a ledger book for 1889 among the files, which listed the Pinkerton income from various cases that year, but there was no mention at all of the Gowen case.

If Linden had twelve of his best men on the case for a week, why was there no income for these men listed? The ledger also listed the supervisors assigned to each particular case, but again there was no mention of any major case in Pennsylvania.

The absence of any documentation could be the result of two possibilities: one the case had been top secret and had been kept off the books; two, Linden had never assigned anyone to the case.

Since Linden had told the press all about the involvement of the Pinkerton Agency in the case, there was no particular reason for secrecy. Therefore, the likely explanation was that Linden had never opened a Gowen file, and his failure to do so must have been based on his knowledge that the Mollys had nothing to do with Gowen's death.

While browsing through the Pinkerton files checking out part of it that referred to Linden, I came across three items that revealed a great deal about the detective, none of which cast a favorable light on his character.

First, there was a press clipping about an interview with Linden, published in the *Times Leader*, a Scranton, PA, newspaper, in December 1889, and in this article he boasts how he got a robber named McCall to turn state's evidence against his two companions in the hope of escaping the hangman's noose. His two companions had fled the country and Linden sweet-talked McCall into making a full confession.

But McCall got the rope as a result of his confession and Linden was smirking when he told the reporter that he thought the rope was far more merciful than life on the run or life in prison. He seemed to enjoy the fact that McCall had died a violent death.

"He sat in that chair where you are sitting," said Linden to the reporter, "and he confessed to everything."

Linden's amusement at how he had doublecrossed McCall and McCall had paid for his faith in Linden by strangling at the end of a rope is chilling to read. Obviously, Linden had a macabre sense of humor and he came across in this instance as a sociopath in his enjoyment of another man's agony.

Linden had used a similar tactic several times during the Molly Maguire trials, when he had frightened members of the AOH into giving evidence under the threat of the hangman's noose. No doubt, he had enjoyed his power to terrorize people back in 1876 and was still enjoying it in the McCall case in 1889.

A far more serious case involving both Linden and Gowen was revealed in a memo Allan Pinkerton wrote to Pinkerton Superintendent George Bangs in the summer of 1875. This involved a conspiracy by Linden, Pinkerton, Bangs and Gowen to set up a vigilante group in the coal regions that would murder Molly Maguire members who were suspected of being involved in violence against the coal barons.

In a hand-written memo Pinkerton ordered Bangs to instruct Linden to organize the vigilante group and to see to it that the group showed no mercy to the Mollys. Pinkerton described Linden as a good man and could be relied on to carry out orders without hesitation. Pinkerton indicated that Bangs should outline the plan to Franklin Gowen, but should not bring Charles Parrish, another coal baron, into the plot for the time being. Pinkerton praised Parrish as a good solid man, but he believed there was no need to bring him on board at that particular time.

Gowen, Parrish and Asa Packer, of Mauch Chunk, were the three major players in the coal regions and had the most to gain in breaking the back of the coal miners union.

Packer and Parrish had stayed discretely on the sidelines while Gowen played the lead role in the war against the unions and the Mollys, but now and again their involvement was revealed and this Pinkerton memo, which mentions Parrish, was such an occasion.

Shortly after this memo was written, a vigilante group attacked an Irish household at Wiggan's Patch, killing a pregnant woman named Ellen McAllister, and her brother Charles O'Donnell, both relatives of AOH leader Jack Kehoe. Two other men were wounded but escaped. O'Donnell had been named by the Pinkertons as a suspect in the Sanger and Uren murders.[119]

However, the murders created such an outrage even among those who did not like the Irish that this particular Pinkerton strategy was not tried again against the Mollys. James McParland was among those who expressed outrage at the killings at Wiggans Patch, and he contacted his supervisors and threatened to resign. However, his fury at the killings was based on the fact that a pregnant woman was killed, not on any opposition to vigilantism by his fellow Pinkertons. The involvement of Linden and Gowen in vigilantism says a number of things about the moral character of both men.

First of all Gowen had supposedly hired the Pinkertons to establish law and order, because he said that the activities of the Molly Maguires, the AOH, and the miners' union - the WBA -were a threat to American democracy. The charge leveled against the Mollys was that they ambushed mine bosses, killing them without warning, and Pinkerton described this activity as comparable to the murders committed by the Thugs, a sect from India who specialized in this type of violence. And he claimed that the Mollys, the AOH and the WBA had conspired with each other to conduct this violence. [120]

[119] Wayne Broehl, *The Molly Maguires.*
[120] Pinkerton, *The Mollie Maguires and the Detective.*

Yet here is a vigilante group, formed on the orders of Allan Pinkerton, who break into a private home... shoot dead a pregnant woman... and then gun down her brother, Charles O'Donnell, killing him with fifteen bullets in the head.

Obviously, Gowen and the Pinkertons were less interested in law and order than they were in defeating violently those that they considered the enemy. This underscores the hypocrisy of the moral posturing of Gowen and other members of the Gowen team during the great Molly Maguire trials that began the following year, when Gowen was to portray himself as the champion of law and order and the Pinkertons as defenders of democracy.

But even though these revelations in the Pinkerton papers were interesting, they shed no light on who had killed Franklin Gowen a dozen years later, or why Linden had gone all out to sell the idea that Gowen's death was a result of suicide.

The revelations do underscore however the viciousness of the Gowen/Pinkerton combo and the thirst for revenge that their activities must have generated among the Irish in the coal regions. Certainly, the relatives of Mrs. McAllister and Charles O'Donnell would have been in an unforgiving mood twelve years later, as would the relatives of twenty other members of the Irish community who went to the gallows as a result of the trials staged-managed by Gowen and Linden.

One wonders what there was about Linden's character that would enable him to organize gangs to commit murder while posing as a police supervisor who was dedicated to protecting the rights of all citizens.

Was there money involved, or did he just enjoy the thrill of life and death power over other men, or his ability to operate entirely outside the law without any fear of prosecution?

Perhaps it was a mixture of both, but it certainly can be said from the McCall case that he enjoyed a hanging.

The Library of Congress papers reveal that Linden left the Pinkertons a year after Gowen's death. He was offered the post of Chief of Detectives in the City of Philadelphia and he quietly departed from the Pinkertons.

For some reason Linden became a name rarely mentioned in the Pinkerton files from that point onward until the 1930s. When Pinkerton Public Relations executives gave interviews about the Molly Maguires to the press during these years his name rarely was mentioned, even though in reality he was *the* Pinkerton agent who was most responsible for destroying the Molly Maguires and the union.

The Pinkerton files reveal that when Linden was offered the job in Philadelphia, the announcement of the offer created an uproar among union members, who viewed Linden as an enemy of trade unions, and he was just as passionately opposed by the ordinary working class, who saw Linden as a capitalist tool. But he had the support of the power brokers in the city and he got the job in spite of the opposition.

One wonders if the departure of Linden from the Pinkertons had anything to do with the Gowen case, or if the fact that his name all but vanished from Pinkerton public relations handouts could be attributed to the unhappiness of the Pinkerton family with the way Linden had handled Gowen's death.

There is no hint of any of this in the files.

The files also contained a comment by James McParland about Gowen's death. In an interview given to a Denver newspaper McParland said he believed that Gowen was involved in a major conflict with the Rockefeller interests and this might have contributed to his death.

More than a hundred years after Gowen's death a member of the Gowen family told me that if Gowen was murdered he would consider the Rockefeller interests a major suspect, and that Linden's collusion with the Rockefellers should not be ruled out either.

My informant was very passionate about his conviction that John D. Rockefeller was in some way responsible for Franklin Gowen's death. He believed he either drove Gowen to suicide or that it was even possible he was involved in his murder -- if Gowen was murdered.

He had also a very low opinion of the Pinkertons, especially of Robert Linden, whom he described as "hired help." He dismissed the reports in the newspapers of the period that Linden was an old friend of the Gowen family, saying that Linden would never have moved in the social circles that Franklin Gowen belonged to and he could never be considered a friend -- he was just a contract employee called in to perform a chore. He also pointed out that the Pinkertons had frequently been hired by the Rockefeller interests, and the Pinkertons could very well have been on the Rockefeller payroll even as Linden was being hired to look into the "suicide" of Franklin Gowen.

"Rockefeller viewed Franklin Gowen as a major threat because he knew exactly the kind of monoply that Rockefeller was creating. He was making major problems for the Rockefellers by challenging them in court, and they did not like it at all. He was a thorn in their side."

There was no proof offered for any of the above, and I viewed it as speculation that might have had no basis in reality. On the other hand, it was possible there was substance to this theory but I had no idea how to go about investigating it. So, I did not pursue the Rockefeller angle even though it was very interesting,

Anyway, the Pinkerton files at the Library of Congress provided no fresh insights into Gowen's death, although the absence of any documentation whatsoever about an official Pinkerton involvement in investigating his death was in itself interesting.

But the papers in this collection were obviously only a fragment of the entire collection and I am sure the papers were heavily edited before they were handed over to the Library of Congress.

An example of the type of editing that must have taken place can be found in the McParland correspondence that is part of the collection. I am sure McParland must have generated hundreds, if not thousands of letters and memos during his career in Denver, but only a score or so have been included here and those that do appear do not show him in a favorable light, because it is very obvious from these documents that the Pinkertons did not think too highly of this nemesis of the Molly Maguires.

Included among the McParland letters are memos from Denver to headquarters in Chicago whining and complaining about his health and about his working conditions, which generated responses from headquarters that suggested that it was time he retired. William Pinkerton tried a soft sell to try to get rid of McParland at first, and then he put pressure on him by appointing a supervisor to whom McParland had to report. Finally, during the last ten years of his career, McParland did not get a single increase in salary, but the detective hung in there anyway and resigned only on his death bed.

Why were all these letters and memos unfavorable to McParland left in the collection for the whole world to see? After all McParland supposedly was a Pinkerton hero whose exploits in Pennsylvania gave the Pinkertons a windfall of favorable publicity.

The reason was probably that McParland was an alcoholic who was a thorn in the side of the Pinkertons for decades, and the presence of the letters was getting some measure of revenge.

But why had they not fired him as far back as the 1890s when the memos first indicated management disenchantment with his personality and his management style? After all, the sons of Allan Pinkerton were very quick to fire other managers who had generated far less animosity. The reality probably was that McParland was privy to too many secrets involving the Pinkerton/Gowen war on the trade unions and the railroading of twenty Irish mine workers to the gallows, and management was afraid he would blow the whistle if he was fired.

I am sure McParland knew all the secrets about Linden forming vigilante groups, and the Pinkerton Agency could not afford to have any of this made public. So, they were stuck with him, and in spite of the fact that William Pinkerton wrote a memo that revealed that management had more problems with McParland than they had with any other manager in the company, and that the Denver Branch made less money than any other branch, McParland was tolerated until death relieved the Pinkertons of the cross they had to bear.

The Pinkerton Papers gave me no clues about who might have been involved in Gowen's death, but the absence of a paper trail did not mean that there had not been documentation in existence at some point in time -- documentation that had been discarded because it was too dangerous to keep around, like most of the documentation involving the Molly Maguires.

The Pinkerton papers did give some insights into the mentality of Franklin Gowen and Robert Linden, however, and revealed them as men who could casually plot murders, and do so without any qualms at all.

However, as far as the basic focus of my research was concerned, I knew that if I were to obtain any new evidence on the Gowen case, I would have to look elsewhere.

There were a number of other archives in the East Coast area that had information on the Molly Maguires, and I decided to touch base with each of them next. One was the Hagley Museum in Wilmington Delaware, which had been provided with a large collection of Molly Maguire-related documents by the Reading Railroad.

Among these documents were reports by Pinkerton agents in the field, including those of Robert Linden, who provided daily reports on their undercover activities among the Mollys. I had reviewed these documents years ago when I was working on *A Molly Maguire Story*, but now I reviewed them again to see if there was anything there about the Gowen case But I was disappointed, there was nothing there at all about Franklin Gowen's death.

The St. Charles Seminary in the Philadelphia area had a collection of correspondence on the Molly Maguires, and I thought I might browse through the archives again, but again there was nothing there of any value. Finally I contacted the Rockefeller Archives in New York for any information available on the Rockefeller relationship with Franklin Gowen, but all I received back was a copy of a letter from Franklin Gowen to John D. Rockefeller, dated August 1889, indicating Gowen intended to subpoena Rockefeller to testify in the upcoming trial in Washington -- the trial Gowen was involved in when he was killed.

This letter hardly seemed a justification for Gowen being murdered by Rockefeller, no matter what others might think.

I had now come to the end of the road as far as research was concerned, without learning who killed Franklin Gowen. This was disappointing.

However, I had proved, at least to my own satisfaction, that Gowen had been murdered, and that a number of people close to him knew who had killed him... and why.

I was well aware, however, that I would lack credibility if I tried to present findings that were based on my judgement alone. I could well imagine my arguments being dismissed because I was not a ballistics expert or a detective or a medical examiner and it would be hard to blame those who came to that conclusion.

After all Gowen's death had taken place in Washington D.C., where many of the nation's leading experts in a whole variety of disciplines were located, and if they voiced few opinions on the blood-stained clothing, then readers might decide that the probability was that my interpretation of this evidence was in some way flawed.

So, I decided that I needed the opinion of a medical examiner or better still medical examiners, and if they agreed that my interpretation of the evidence was not in error, then I could argue that Gowen had been murdered.

After I decided that I would seek professional advice on this project, my problem would be to find professionals willing to get involved in the project.

I did not for a moment think that getting recruits would be an easy matter, but I intended to give it a try anyway.

A NEED FOR EXPERT OPINION

Once I decided that I was going to seek professional opinion on the evidence I had gathered on the Gowen case, I could think of a number of reasons why professional medical examiners would find it a problem getting involved, especially since the end result would be printed in a book. They would have a question about the accuracy of the information I was providing them; they would worry about the context in which I would use any information provided by them; and there would be a concern about getting involved with an amateur in a project like this in the first place.

Before I approached any of these professionals, however, I had to decide how much information I should make available to them, and what type of opinions I hoped to get from these professionals.

I decided that the best I could hope for was that one or all of them would state that based on the evidence I had provided that it seemed evident that Franklin Gowen had not committed suicide. And in addition, I hoped that they would conclude, as I had, that the body had been moved after death, but before it was "discovered" by Wormley.

I took a long time to decide what information I should provide that would enable them to come to a conclusion.

Should I dump all the material I had gathered in their lap? Or be highly selective about what I sent on to them?

The thing I wanted to avoid at all costs was to "try the case" by arguing for my point of view. I thought it would be much better to provide an objective account of the evidence that confronted Linden and Coroner Patterson, without editorial comment, and let them take it from there.

After thinking about the matter for some time, I decided there was no point in letting them know up front about the contradictions involving the gun, or the theories about bankruptcy or temporary insanity.

Eventually, I decided that I would only send them information that was open to contradiction or more than one interpretation, and then ask if this evidence pointed toward murder or suicide.

But first I had to find medical examiners who were willing to cooperate with me, and I started a methodical search of those doctors in the northeast who had expertise in this discipline.

I had very little illusions about this being an easy matter. I knew that not one of them would be at ease in putting their name on an opinion in a published book when they had no first hand evidence of the crime scene.

I got around this problem by telling them that all I wanted was their opinion and that I would not name them in the book at all, so they need not feel uneasy about this issue.

But I met with a total lack of interest in any medical examiner to get involved in the project until I got influential friends, who knew three of them, to intercede on my behalf, and then and only then did I get the cooperation I needed.

Two of the experts were practicing medical examiners, one in Connecticut and one in New Jersey; the third was a retired medical examiner from New Jersey.

Each promised to give an opinion based on what I had provided them, but all three made it very clear that since they had no first hand knowledge of the crime scene, and I, for that matter had no first hand knowledge either, that they definately would not want to have their names associated with the project.

Since I had been expecting this attitude anyway, and my goal was to get second opinions not testimonials, I agreed to these conditions. Each in turn then asked for a written description of the evidence.

The following is the summary of the evidence I sent to each medical examiner.

THE DEATH OF FRANKLIN GOWEN

Franklin Gowen was found dead in an hotel room in Washington D.C. on Saturday, December 14, 1889.

He was one of the best known businessmen in the United States and his death created a national sensation.

THE BODY

Gowen's body was stretched out flat on its back in front of a mirror hung over the fireplace;

a 38mm Smith & Wesson pistol lay on the floor near his right hand;

a bullet had entered his head above and behind the right ear and exited through the left ear;

the entrance wound was clean: there was no evidence of burn or powder marks;

his shirt, jacket and underwear were soaked with blood;

the handle of the gun was covered with blood, but not the barrel.

The carpet, beneath the head, had blood stains; the only other blood spots were several small spots on the marble fireplace, and a blob of blood near a bureau, fifteen feet to the right of the body.

No one in the hotel had claimed to have heard the gunshot that killed Gowen.

The last person to see Gowen alive was a hotel maid who wanted to clean the room at 3:30 PM and found Gowen writing at a table. Gowen told her he was busy and told her to come back later. She came back at 4:30 PM and at 6 PM but found the door locked and no response to her knocks.

Gowen's body was found by the hotel's owner the next day at noon. The coroner estimated that death had taken place seven hours before the body's discovery.

RELATED INFORMATION

The door of the bedroom was locked from the inside; however, there was another locked door leading from the bathroom of the suite to the corridor. The bathroom door had a Yale-type lock that could be locked from the outside, but could be opened from the inside by turning a knob. A key to this door was in the hotel office

The drapes and curtains on the windows were drawn.

A gas reading light that had stood on a table was on the floor, unlit.

A chair was also overturned.

The owner of the hotel called the police after the body was discovered and within an hour he had the body wrapped in a sheet and sent to the New Jersey Avenue Police Station. The owner of the hotel then proceeded to pull up the carpet and pull the wallpaper from the wall. This happened before the coroner arrived.

The coroner eventually arrived and interviewed the hotel owner and viewed the body at the police station. He then issued a verdict on the cause of death: it was his opinion that since the bedroom door was locked from the inside Gowen's death was a suicide-- that Gowen had held a gun close to his head and pulled the trigger. He stated that an inquest was unnecessary. An inquest was not held.

VERDICT DISPUTED

The coroner's verdict was disputed by an assistant district attorney, as well as by a captain in the Washington police, and a doctor who was a resident in the hotel.

The assistant district attorney said that he did not see how the coroner could arrive at a verdict of suicide, given the wounds on the head. The resident doctor -- Dr. Porter -- said he was the first to view the body, and the right side of Gowen's face was smeared with smoke and gun powder.

The resident doctor said he did not see how the wound could be self-inflicted.

The police captain said it was impossible for Gowen to hold a gun in a position that would inflict wounds of a type found on Gowen's head.

Other questions that were unanswered include the following:

1... The handle of the gun was covered in blood. How did the blood get on the handle and not on the barrel?

2... Gowen's shirt, waistcoat and underclothes were soaked in blood. The blood on this part of his body seemed to defy gravity, since most of it had not drained from the head *down to* the carpet but *across or upwards* toward the chest and waist.

3.... Why had the hotel owner been in such a hurry to remove the wallpaper and the carpet?

4.... Why had the coroner rushed to a verdict without an autopsy?

*

In a cover letter I informed them that I was not including information that did not bear directly on the principal issue, namely, if Gowen's death was the result of murder or suicide.

It took time for the medical examiners to respond but when they did, their responses ranged from a brief one-paragraph comment to a lengthy telephone call that discussed every aspect of the case. I was intrigued with the results.

The Connecticut coroner was very cautious about drawing any conclusions. He stated that the "material is interesting and it certainly raises questions."

But, he stated, in the absence of source materials it "is impossible to independently review any of these diagnosis and incorporate them into any sort of thinking."

However, he then went on to make the following statement: "If all the diagnoses that are made are taken at face value, the very least we can say is that the body was moved before these observations were made. Since there is a recorded history of the body being moved and the scene, rather profoundly disturbed between the time of its so called discovery and the definitive analysis by the coroner, it is highly likely that the scene was also disturbed before any 'observations were made' by anyone."

The medical examiner's opinions were stated very briefly, but they focused on an issue that had been the cornerstone of my own argument: that the body had been moved and the death scene disturbed prior to Wormley "discovering" the body.

The New Jersey medical examiner said that Gowen must have been sitting in a chair when he was shot and must have remained sitting in the chair for some time after the wound was inflicted because this was the only way to explain the amount of blood on his coat and waistcoat.

I thought this was very interesting because it suggested perhaps that whoever shot him had left the body as it was and simply left the room. If this was true, then some other person or persons would have entered the room and rearranged the body. This agreed with one of the scenarios I mentioned earlier -- namely, members of the hotel staff had rearranged the body to make it look like suicide.

The New Jersey medical examiner also stated that the absence of any burns or tattooing around the wound ruled out suicide. He dismissed Coroner Patterson's claim that if the pistol were pressed closely to the skull there would be no burn marks on the skin.

The New Jersey Medical examiner said the heat of the rim of the muzzle would definitely have left a burn mark.

In conclusion, he said the available evidence provided by me, if accurate, would suggest murder not suicide as a cause of death.

But, he cautioned, this opinion was based on my evidence only, and he would never come to any conclusion about a case such as this until he had first hand knowledge of all the facts involved. He said he was just providing an opinion based on secondary sources.

I did not blame these two practicing medical examiners for being very cautious about the statements they made, because they were not dealing with forensic evidence that they could examine. So, over and over again they would say -- if the so called evidence is taken at face value, then this is my reaction to it, but I cannot say for sure that the evidence you presented is evidence that can be relied on because you are getting it second hand or third hand also.

I thought that was fair enough.

The retired medical examiner, also from New Jersey, was more relaxed and much more willing to speculate on what had happened to Franklin B. Gowen.

First of all, he stated that the body had definitely been moved after Gowen's death, and he had more than one reason for this opinion.

According to him, the blood could not have soaked Gowen's clothes unless he had been sitting in a chair -- an opinion that confirmed the opinion of the other two experts -- but he also raised the possibility that Gowen had been shot in the chest. He asked me if there had been any mention of a chest wound and I said I knew nothing about this.

Then he said that the way the body had been lying on the floor was, in his opinion, not the way that the body would have been laid out if Gowen stood in front of a mirror and shot himself.

The medical examiner said that if Gowen had shot himself while standing up, he would immediately have lost consciousness and he would, in the vast majority of such instances, have pitched *forward*, landing on his face and chest.

The medical examiner said he had seen scores of such suicides and the body had almost always crumpled into a heap in this manner, and even though he did not rule out the possibility that the body fell backwards, he said the body could never have landed in the tidy configuration it was found in: legs and arms neatly arranged.

The blood on the handle of the gun also interested him. He believed that it could only have got there if the gun had been lying in a pool of blood, but since there was no pool of blood where the gun lay on the carpet and no reason why it should have been there, this was one more indication that the body had been moved. He said in all probability the gun had initially been on the floor beneath the chair and the blood had dripped down onto the gun after soaking Gowen's clothes. The retired coroner said no other theory made any sense.

He went on to say that if he had been the coroner on the scene the first thing he would have checked out would be the possibility that more than one bullet had been fired.

He said the reason for that would have been the amount of blood on Gowen's chest, and also the fact that the wallpaper had been ripped off and the carpet ripped up.

"Somebody was hiding something," he said.

There was obviously a conspiracy going on here, he continued, and he believed it had to involve some of the hotel staff. As far as the coroner being involved, he thought that it was possible that the coroner was not a doctor at all, or he may have been just incompetent.

"At that time, in the 19th century, many of the coroners were elected to the position and were not really qualified to do the job."

The retired medical examiner had a few other comments to make that was relevant to the case.

On the question of the bullet wound, he was convinced it could not have been self-inflicted because of the absence of burn marks around the entrance wound; he dismissed Coroner Patterson's theory that the pistol had been held tightly against the head to explain the absence of burn marks.

"There would have been a neat little red circle at the entrance wound if this had happened," he said.

This medical examiner knew nothing about the Molly Maguires and did not know anything about reasons for Gowen's murder.

"But usually in these types of cases the first thing a detective would investigate if there is a suspicion of murder is who had the reason and the opportunity to commit the crime. It seems amazing that the investigation was so brief -- that it was left in the hands of a private investigator -- and that the investigator should have had the final say on what went down in that hotel bedroom. Really amazing."

I could not agree with him more. There were many aspects of the Gowen case I found amazing, and the most amazing aspect of all was that the case was allowed to go cold without anyone mounting a serious challenge about the suicide verdict that had been arrived at in December of 1889.

*

THE LAST WORD

I had now arrived at the point where I seemed to have nothing further to investigate, and I was a little disappointed that I had not unearthed an iota of information that might have given me a clue to who had killed Franklin Gowen.

I reviewed the material I had acquired one more time to see if there was anything I had missed. During the review I came up with an item that I had decided to investigate, but had never got around to conducting the investigation. The item involved the administration of the estate of Franklin Gowen, which, according to the *Philadelphia Inquirer,* had been filed for probate several days after Gowen's death by Francis Gowen.

On the question about the probate of the Gowen estate, when I first read the item in the *Inquirer* I wondered why Francis Innes Gowen had been in such a hurry to file for letters of administration. The letters of administration had been filed less than forty-eight hours after Gowen had been found dead, and a day before he had been buried at Mount Airy Cemetary.

The distribution of Franklin Gowen's assets were not of much interest to me initially, because I assumed that these assets would be turned over to his wife and daughter.

But when I became convinced that Gowen was murdered and that his estate was worth $450,000, which would be millions of dollars in today's currency, I thought it might be worth while to "follow the money" to see just who got what amount of money when Francis Innes Gowen divided up the assets.

There should be no reason why Gowen's wife and daughter had not inherited the entire estate, but the only way to find out for sure would be to examine the documents involved in the administration process.Apart from a curiosity about how the assetts were distributed, I wondered why there had not been an extensive search for Gowen's will which had been known to exist.

In documents filed on Monday December 16, Francis Innes Gowen stated that Gowen's papers were searched the previous day but neither he or his staff were able to locate the will, so, with the agreement of Mrs. Gowen and her daughter, he had filed for permission to administer the estate.

I wondered if this was standard procedure in 1889 -- to make a quick search for a will, which had existed, and when it could not be found, to immediately file letters of administration, all within forty-eight hours of Gowen's death. The haste seemed unusual, and the reason could not be determined.

The Petition requesting that Francis I. Gowen and James Hood be named administrators of the estate was signed by Frederick Gowen, Franklin's brother, Esther B. Gowen, his wife, Esther Gowen, his daughter, and Ellen Gowen, his sister. The Letters were granted. There were a number of conditions attached to the Letters of Administration: the administrators had to place notices in the newspapers inviting creditors to file claims, a full and detailed listing of the assets had to be provided within 30 days, and within one year there had to be a complete accounting on the distribution of all the assets. All the material had to be filed with the court.

I was interested in all the material generated by the administration process because I thought it might yield some information relevant to Franklin Gowen's death. For instance, in spite of reviewing the Pinkerton archives I could not find any information on how Robert Linden had been compensated for his time on the Franklin Gowen case and I thought his name might appear on the list of creditors.

Then, I was aware that Francis Innes Gowen had inherited his uncle's law practice in which he had been a junior partner, and I wondered if there had been any mention of the transfer of the practice to Francis Innes in the administration documents.

Finally, I wanted to know exactly what Gowen was worth and who inherited the money, and only the documents filed with the court within the one-year period would reveal this information. The Petition had only provided an estimate, and the real amount could be far below or far above that amount.

The only documentation I had requested initially from the Philadelphia Register of Wills was a copy of the Petition, which was supplied to me after I requested it.

However, I decided that I should take a look at all the documents in the file and I forwarded the required fees and requested a copy of everything in the Gowen file -- only to be told that the three-page Petition was all there was in the Gowen file. There was no list of creditors, no breakdown of assets, no description of how the assets had been distributed.

Since I was convinced that Francis Innes Gowen would have to have complied with all the requirements stated in the Petition in order to get a judge to sign off on the Gowen estate, and that the documents involved in this process must have been sent to the judge for his review, then the question was where had these documents gone if they were not in the same file with the Petition.

One would assume that all relevant documents would have been kept in the one file, and they should have remained in that file once the judge had reviewed them.

I contacted the Register of Wills again and informed the staff that the documents I had requested had not been provided and would they check the archives again to see if the requested material had been misfiled.

I received a reply that stated that the Gowen Estate had a file number, A 1326--1889, and that the only documents in this file were the Petition. I followed up with several calls to the Register of Wills office, but in the end I had to face the fact that the Gowen Estate files were no longer available.

It seems that the Gowen files, like the police files in Washington involving Gowen's death, the Washington coroner's files, and the Pinkerton files that dealt with the Gowen investigation were gone with the wind.

I was tempted to view the absence of all these files as an indication that the files had been deliberately stolen in order to remove a paper trail, but I had no evidence to support such a theory, and there could very well be a reasonable explanation for the absence of such files.

But I was suspicious nevertheless, because in my research for *A Molly Maguire Story* I discovered that critical files were missing at key points in my research and the pattern was so pronounced that I had come to the conclusion at the time that the files had been deliberately "mislaid."

The missing probate files, however, served as the end of my research into who had killed Franklin Gowen. I had documented the fact that he had not committed suicide, but I had been unable to prove who killed him or whether the killing was accidental or deliberate

I also documented the fact that the true nature of Gowen's death was covered up without a great deal of expertise.

The circumstances surrounding Gowen's death has remained a mystery for more than a hundred years, and if the true nature of his death is ever revealed, it will require the introduction of new evidence, not available at present.

END

BIBLIOGRAPHY

PRIMARY SOURCES

Newspapers

The Mauch Chunk Democrat
The Mauch Chunk Gazette
The Miners' Journal (Pottsville)
The New York Herald
The New York Times
The Philadelphia Inquirer
The Pottsville Republican
The Star, Washington
The Evening Star, Washington
The Times Leader(Scranton)

Manuscript Collections

St. Charles of Borromeo Seminary, Overbrook, Pa.
Molly Maguire Collection
Papers of Archbishop Wood

Hagley Museum and Library, Wilmington, Delaware
Philadelphia & Reading Railroad Collection
Historical Information, Molly Maguire Papers
Stenographic Reports of the trials of John Donohue, Patrick
Hester, Martin Bergin, James McDonnell

Library of Congress, Washington, D.C.
Pinkerton Manuscript Collection

BOOKS

Broehl, Wayne. *The Molly Maguires.* 1964.
Campbell, Patrick. *A Molly Maguire Story, 1992.*
Friedman, Morris. *The Pinkerton Labor Spy. Wilshire Books, 1907.*
Kenny, Kevin. *Making Sense of the Molly Maguires.* Oxford. 1998.
Lukas, J. Anthony. *Big Trouble. 1997.*
Pinkerton, Allan. *The Molly Maguires and the Detectives. 1877.*
Schlegel, Marvin W. *Ruler of the Reading: The Life of Franklin B. Gowen. 1947.*
Siringo, Charles. *Two Evil Isms: Pinkertonism and Anarchism.* 1913

SECONDARY SOURCES

BOOKS

Bimba, Anthony. *The Molly Maguires.* 1932
Coleman, James Walter.*The Molly Maguire Riots. 1936*
Dewees, Francis P. *The Molly Maguires:* Origins, Growth, and Character of the Organization. 1877.
Eveland & Harris. *The Molly Maguires.* 1876.
Korson, George. *Minstrels of the Mine Patch.* 1938
Lucy, Ernest W. *The Mollie Maguires of Pennsylvania. 1882.*
McCarthy, Charles. *The Great Molly Maguire Hoax.* 1969.
Wallace, Anthony. *St. Clair.*

RELATED SUBJECTS

Aurand, Harold. *From the Molly Maguires to the United Mine Workers. 1971.*

Foner, Phillip. *History of the Labor Movement in the United States 1947.*

Horan, James David. *The Pinkertons: The Detective Dynasty That Made History.1968*

Lens, Sydney. *The Labor Wars: From the Mollie Maguires to the Sitdowns. 1973.*

Long, Priscilla. *Where the Sun Never Shines. 1989.*

INDEX

OTHER BOOKS BY PATRICK CAMPBELL

A Molly Maguire Story. 1992. $13.95.
An investigation into the arrest, trial and execution of accused Molly Maguire leader Alec Campbell. Alec Campbell was the author's great uncle.

Memories of Dungloe. 1993. $11.95.
The author describes growing up in northwest Donegal, Ireland, in the 1940s and 1950s.

Death in Templecrone. 1995. $11.95
A description of the Irish famine as it ravaged northwest Donegal, 1845-50.

Methuselah. 1997. $11.95.
Fiction. A serial killer is loose in the Hills of Donegal.

Tunnel Tigers. 2000. $13.95.
A description of the author's experience driving tunnels through the mountains of Scotland in the 1950s.

Shipping at book rate: $1.50

ALL BOOKS AVAILABLE THROUGH .... P.H. CAMPBELL, 82 BENTLEY AVE, JERSEY CITY, NJ 07304. 201 434 2432. PATHCAMPBE@AOL.COM

A Molly Maguire Story
by Patrick Campbell

On June 21, 1877, ten Irish-Americans were executed in the mining areas of Pennsylvania. All were accused of being members of a terrorist group called the Molly Maguires, and all were convicted of planning and carrying out the murder of a number of mining officials. Ten more Irish-Americans were executed in Pennsylvania in the next 18 months on the same charges. One of the men executed on June 21, 1877, was Alexander Campbell, grand-uncle of the author.

The Molly Maguire executions generated a great deal of controversy in Pennsylvania from the 1870s to the present, with Irish-Americans claiming the Mollies were framed by the mine owners, while other ethnic groups believe that they were guilty as charged and deserved the punishment they received.

The author first heard about the execution of his grand-uncle back in the late 1940s in Dungloe, County Donegal, Ireland, and in the early 1970s, while living in New Jersey, began a fifteen-year investigation into the entire Molly Maguire controversy in order to determine if Alexander Campbell was guilty or innocent.

A Molly Maguire Story is an account of that investigation.

"A frightening tale of a perverted legal system"—Irish Echo

"A dark page in Irish-American history"—Celtic News Service

"An eye-opening expose" —Jersey Journal

"An eye-opener"—Citizens' Voice, Wilkes-Barre

Published by
P. H. Campbell
82 Bentley Avenue
Jersey City, NJ 07304
(201) 434-2432

$13.95

ISBN 0-681-82875-7

MEMORIES OF DUNGLOE

- Memories of Dungloe, County Donegal, in the 1940s and 1950s.
- An old Molly Maguire dies in Dungloe 70 years after the hangman claimed his brother in Mauch Chunk, Pennsylvania.
- A German spy masquerading as a Dutch woman is arrested.
- Many young men leave to go off to fight in the foreign wars and never come back.
- Innisfree - an island paradise for children.
- Protestants and Catholics - an uneasy coexistence.
- Ghosts, superstitions and offbeat characters.

"MEMORIES HAS THE POWER TO CAUSE US TO WEEP, REJOICE, FEAR, OR SADLY REMEMBER THE PAST. OUR MEMORIES ARE THE TREASURE-TROVE OF OUR LIVES -- TO BE SHARED CAUTIOUSLY WITH TRUSTED FRIENDS. PATRICK CAMPBELL HAS HONORED US WITH THIS TRUST, AND ENRICHED US WITH HIS MEMOIRS."

- Kevin O'Neill Shanley, Celtic News Service

"A UNIQUE AND FASCINATING ACCOUNT OF GROWING UP IN DONEGAL IN THE '40S AND '50S. SOMETIMES COMIC, SOMETIMES TRAGIC, SOMETIMES SHOCKING. ALWAYS INTERESTING."

- Angela Carter, Irish Books and Graphics

"CAMPBELL SHAPES HIS MEMOIR AS A COAT OF MANY COLORS, INVITING THE READER TO BE WARMED BY THE PEOPLE OF DUNGLOE AND THE PERMUTATIONS OF THEIR LIVES. JUST LOVELY"

- Claire Grimes, Publisher, *The Irish Echo*

$11.95

ISBN 0-9637701-0-1

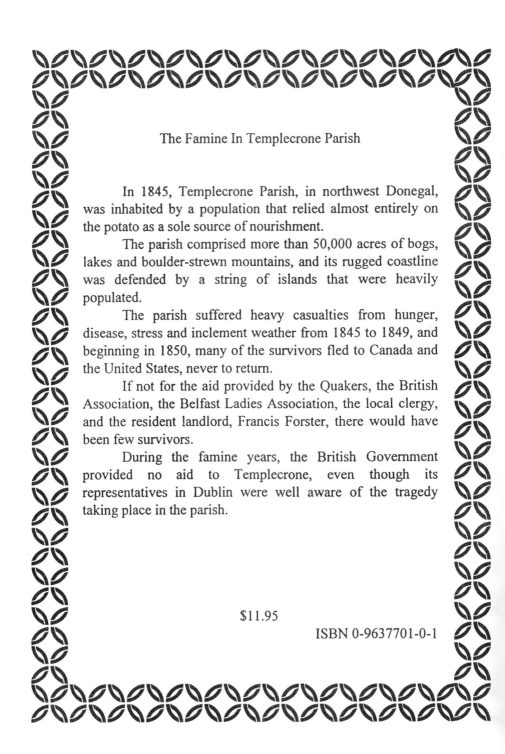

The Famine In Templecrone Parish

In 1845, Templecrone Parish, in northwest Donegal, was inhabited by a population that relied almost entirely on the potato as a sole source of nourishment.

The parish comprised more than 50,000 acres of bogs, lakes and boulder-strewn mountains, and its rugged coastline was defended by a string of islands that were heavily populated.

The parish suffered heavy casualties from hunger, disease, stress and inclement weather from 1845 to 1849, and beginning in 1850, many of the survivors fled to Canada and the United States, never to return.

If not for the aid provided by the Quakers, the British Association, the Belfast Ladies Association, the local clergy, and the resident landlord, Francis Forster, there would have been few survivors.

During the famine years, the British Government provided no aid to Templecrone, even though its representatives in Dublin were well aware of the tragedy taking place in the parish.

$11.95

ISBN 0-9637701-0-1

The Last Days of Oscar Devenney

In May 1973, a teacher named Oscar Devenney, who taught in a parochial school in Greystones, County Donegal, suddenly acquired the ability to heal serious diseases. He also acquired the ability to read minds and to forsee the future.

Devenney's ability to heal those who were seriously ill made him immensely popular, but his ability to read the minds of all those he came in contact with struck fear into the hearts of those who had skeletons in the family closet, and these people crossed the street when they saw Devenney coming.

The resident of Greystones who felt most threatened by the teacher's unusual abilities was a very old man known as Methuselah, who had been killing people in the Greystones area for many years but who had always escaped detection because he made the murders look like accidents or death by natural causes.

But now all Oscar Devenney had to do was to look Methuselah in the eye and he would know exactly what the old man was, so the stage was set for a bloody confrontation between the psychic and the serial killer.

$11.95

TUNNEL TIGERS

Tunnel tigers belong to an elite group of construction workers who specialize in a highly paid but dangerous profession: driving tunnels through mountains or underneath rivers or other large bodies of water, on locations as far apart as Sydney, Australia, and San Francisco. At the turn of the last century, they tunneled out the subways under New York and London; in the 1930s, they worked on the Holland and Lincoln tunnels that link New York and New Jersey; and in the 1940s and 1950s, they were involved in a score of huge hydroelectric tunnels in the Highlands of Scotland. They continue with their dangerous craft today in various locations all over the world.

Many of these daring men were born in northwest Donegal, Ireland, where the tunnel tigers were viewed as local folk heroes because they had the bravado to work in dangerous working conditions that few other working men could endure.

The author worked as a tunnel tiger for four years in Scotland, before emigrating to the United States and taking up less lucrative but less dangerous professions.

Tunnel Tigers provides a colorful portrait of scores of off-beat characters who worked on the Scottish projects, and of the tensions that were created when men of various religious and ethnic groups shared the same space.

*

I found the book of absorbing interest and read it straight through in one reading .... Eric McKeever, Publisher, Anthracite History Journal, and Author, Tales of the Mine Country.

*

Brilliant. Moving. Memorable ... stories that stay with you for life ... Christine Goldbeck, author, A Tribute to O'Hara and Other Stories.

*

A poignant, gripping story --Howard Crown, author, Guide to the Molly Maguires.

$13.95   ISBN 0-9637701-1-X